A NEW YOU

COOKBOOK

A DAILY WEIGHT MANAGEMENT PROGRAM

By Pat S McCarthy

FORWARD BY:

Dr. John C. Stady

LIC: 95-068062

ISBN: 0-9646711-0-7

IN MEMORY OF_____

This book is written in the memory of

BILL SWANK

my brother

who lost his life at the age of 26
January 27, 1994

a tragic death.

ALWAYS REMEMBERED

NEVER FORGOTTEN

DEDICATION

To everyone out there: Who is taking that first and most important step to better themselves by changing their lifestyle to a healthier way of life...

This book is also dedicated to anyone and everyone: Who has encouraged me and given me support throughout the making of this book...

To my mother: Who's given me the love and support through all the crazy ideas I've ever had over the years. You've never thought them to be anything less than experience and growth.

To Dana Fragakis: An angel sent from heaven. The love, strength, and support given at the most difficult time in my life, through my brother's death. You gave me the strength.

FORWARD

With todays' ever increasing speed of life, we tend to dismiss the importance of our health. There are periods when we must slow down, look around and reassess where we are going. This manual can be a guide to give you direction as well as make you ask more questions in gaining ever increasing health.

Dr. John C. Stady

This is not a book about weight loss. It is a piece of Pat Swank McCarthy herself. It is a result of her years of training, self teaching, listening and learning.

This is a manual on how to change how you think. This manual will help you with training, eating, thinking, and achieving whatever your personal goals are.

I have known Pat for some time. She is one of the most sincere and caring people I have known. I wish her the best, as I wish you the best in achieving your health goals.

PREFACE_____

As our world is changing so quickly, so are our eating habits. As adults, it's important that we stick to healthy eating patterns, so that we may pass healthy habits on to our children, giving them the best head start with their lives, balancing our lifestyle, and eating to the best of our knowledge for a long and happy life.

This book is to give you an idea of how to start your healthier NEW YOU. It is not intended as a medical program, or to replace any program your physician may have you on, it is only a guide. I always recommend that you check with your physician before starting any new program. This is a guide to give you the mental and physical basics to eat healthy, along with having fun with new recipes, adding to them or changing them to your liking.

The data collected throughout this book is through experience, trainers, nutrition classes, and an enormous amount of time spent researching recipes that are not only healthy and balanced, but low-fat and flavorful. It also contains opinions from nutritionists and professionals in the medical field.

Have fun with it! Take the knowledge that you want with you and pass it on so that everyone can help make our future, along with our children's futures, a healthy one.

ACKNOWLEDGMENTS _____

Acknowledgments are hard. I know that I'll forget someone, and EVERYONE is so important. I do thank everyone, though.

I first want to thank my HIGHER POWER for giving me the confidence and faith to FINALLY BELIEVE IN ME, as this is the first step I believe, to a happy healthy life.

Thanks to my first personal trainer MARK BORDCOSH for the support and confidence when I was at my heaviest. You brought me to a level I thought I could never reach. To compete in a bodybuilding competition was a dream I had come true. I've been able to start a healthy life because of you.

I would like to thank EVERYONE involved in making this book at all possible:

STEVE SANDBURG & PAT McCARTHY: Illustrations

KIYOTO HARA: Book cover and design

MARK BORDCOSH: Workout Delivery

DR. JOHN STADY: Medical advice and forward

JUDEE NORDBY: Book Formatting

PATTI WONG: Editing

Thanks to my FAMILY and FRIENDS who have put up with all my past crazy projects over the years, for supporting me in this one, and listening to me talk about it all the time.

A special thanks to DR. JOHN STADY for his patience in allowing me to constantly ask medical and health related questions, going beyond his duty as a doctor, by taking the time to answer and make sure I understood. You deserve a medal for this one.

Last, but never the least, to all my nutrition educators, a very big thank you. Without you I would have NEVER learned the proper way to eat and maintain a healthy eating lifestyle. I would have probably continued the yo-yo dieting syndrome for years to come. EDUCATION IS POWER!

TO EVERYONE, A HUGE THANK YOU!

*CONGRATULATIONS*_____

You've taken the first step to a NEW YOU. You will find this cookbook different than any other cookbook you've ever bought. This book will not only help you, but also show you how to give yourself a new look from the outside, as well as the inside. This is for ANYONE, whether you are trying to lose weight, gain weight, watch your cholesterol, or just want to improve your eating habits. A NEW YOU is for you!

This cookbook is unique in the sense that it not only teaches you the basics on what to eat, but how to prepare it. Also, it is motivational. The aim is to help you look INSIDE yourself as to why you have the eating habits you do, how to break the old patterns and help you set new and healthy patterns for yourself. This is the mental aspect of good nutrition that seems to get missed in other programs. You may change your physique from the outside, but to maintain it you will have to change inside, too. The key to a new you is to BELIEVE IN YOURSELF, HAVE CONFIDENCE YOU CAN DO IT, and most importantly, LOVE YOURSELF! This guide will help you in those stages to come.

To help you better understand the dynamics of the nutrition guide, I have incorporated a VISUAL theme (we humans are such visual beings), relating to: How to feed, ride and maintain a horse. Like the progress towards A NEW YOU needs to be taken step by step, a horse and rider need to take it step by step. When we come to the end you will have learned how to maintain the NEW YOU through the years to come.

I'm so excited for you, so let's get going and have some fun!

I strongly recommend before starting any fitness or eating program, that you consult your physician. Remember, each person is different and what works for others may not necessarily work for you. We want to optimize what's best for you and SAFEST for you.

INTRODUCTION

Let me tell you a little of how and why this cookbook all got started.

*I always had the famous label known as "**CHUBBY**" that so many of us had when we were younger. In my mid twenties I had hit an all time high of 200 plus pounds. I'm only 5'3" so every bit of the 200 pounds showed. I was now a "CHUBBY" adult. That's putting it mildly. Ha, I was just plain **FAT!** I used to hate that word.*

In 1984 I had a true eye opener. I had some surgery done, and when the surgeon wrote in his report and talked to me about the procedure, he didn't use the word "fat", he used the word "OBESE". I NEVER considered myself obese, even though I knew I was fat. I became angry and my heart sank. My self esteem grew worse. I then decided to DIET (this is a word you will learn to omit from your vocabulary, as you will never try another so-called DIET again). I tried every diet known to man, and did the "yo-yo" diet for years, with little success I may add.

After years of beating myself down due to the continuing weight problem, I decided to "Get on a horse of a different color," and try a whole new approach to losing the weight. I joined a gym! I have always admired how bodybuilders physiques seem to look so healthy, and thought that maybe they held the key to getting fit and staying fit. Going into the gym I was totally intimidated. Walk in there in shorts? I wouldn't have even CONSIDERED those skimpy suits some women wore. When I imagined myself in one, I burst out laughing. Sound familiar? I had no idea how to start. I was overwhelmed and confused. I tried a few weeks of doing it on my own, but knowing myself all too well, I realized if I didn't get someone to teach me I would get bored, lose interest, fall back into my old ways and be back to square one again. I scouted out a trainer. I can't tell you what I was looking for in a trainer; I didn't even have a clue, and had little money to work with.

I found a trainer who, during his interview, asked me where I wanted to be in the future with my weight. I hesitantly, thinking he would laugh, told him, "I've always dreamt of competing in a body building competition." HE DIDN'T LAUGH! He just said, "That's possible, we can shoot for it." We trained and ate, trained and ate, trained and ate. Yes, I said, "Ate and ate and ate." NOT STARVE AND STARVE AND STARVE! After about nine months of hard work, he made me pick an upcoming competition to enter that was at least six months away. I thought he was out of his mind, but did as I was told.

When six months came and I found myself half naked in one of those tiny bikinis that barely covers anything, in a room filled with competitors stepping on the scale to weigh in with the rest of them. I thought of myself as a SHY, FAT girl among all these fit, athletic bodies. I figured I was crazy! But then, for the first time I looked in the mirror and saw my reflection different than I'd seen it before. I was amazed, thrilled and excited! I experienced a feeling of self accomplishment in becoming one of "Them", the body builders. When I stepped onto the stage to do my routine, I thanked the Lord above. My dream had come true.

Fear set in right after the competition as I realized a total transformation had taken place. I ate again out of fear and began putting the weight back on. I knew just how happy and healthy I was with myself when I was eating and exercising properly. The old ways were only destructive. I turned right back around and "went back" to the new life I had just made for myself.

The recipes in this book came about as I learned to cook and change my eating habits through training. I couldn't find good cookbooks that had any real flavor. When they did have flavor, they contained too much sugar, or something else I was trying to eliminate. Friends kept asking for my advice on eating and recipes, and I gladly handed them out. Many people asked why I didn't write a cookbook, but at the time I didn't think much about it. Well, guess what? The idea became a reality. Another dream came true? These recipes are intended to help you learn, or continue to eat healthy, balanced, low-fat, and in some cases, SUGAR FREE FOR DIABETICS. The recipes are also a GUIDE for you, so that you can add and change other recipes to suit your needs.

This is how this "chubby" and "obese" person turned out. I hope you have enjoyed the story, and can find something similar in your life. I hope you will tell your own success story to me one day.

Before   **After**

TABLE OF CONTENTS

SECTION I: RECIPES FOR THE MIND
MENTAL PREPARATION

SECTION II: RECIPES FOR THE HEART
DYNAMICS OF HEALTHY EATING

SITTING ON THE HORSE

SECTION III: RECIPES FOR THE SOUL

COOKBOOK SECTION

1. SOUPS AND SALADS

2. POULTRY

Turkey

Chicken

3. SEAFOOD

4. BEEF

5. GRAINS

6. PASTAS AND RICE

7. VEGETABLE DISHES

8. SWEETS AND SNACKS

9. BEVERAGES

10. SAUCES, DIPS AND MISCELLANEOUS

SECTION IV: QUICK REFERENCES

RIDING INTO THE SUNSET

SADDLING UP

Psychology of Healthy Eating

One of the first misconceptions people have about lowering their weight is to eat less. If a person decides to do this, this is known to your body as a starvation mode, and the body immediately thinks to store what it has because it's not getting fed, therefore making it much more difficult for you to lose weight. The body stores the fat in order to use it later to survive. The concept of cutting food from your daily diet doesn't work. DIETS DON'T WORK! The word DIET will no longer exist in your vocabulary. It is important to EAT, and learn good nutrition, so that your body can function properly, and keep you healthy.

What is the next thing that a person does when the're trying to lose weight? THINK THEY ARE ALWAYS HUNGRY. Which is probably true because again, the body thinks it's starving. Your body's metabolism is such a magnificent device. Learning how this works, will open your eyes to why DIETS don't work and eating does. Every person's metabolism responds in different ways, what may work for another person, may NOT work for you.

1

What's the third thing that happens on a diet? Maybe stepping on that little machine in your bathroom all too often to see just how many pounds you lost.   THROW THAT THING AWAY! Yes, your scale. Regulating your weight loss only by the scale isn't accurate. If it hasn't changed you get depressed, you feel frustrated, and maybe even decide to give up.   The scale doesn't indicate WHAT you've lost, in Water, Muscle, or Fat. With proper nutrition and exercise, most likely you will lose fat at an even pace and not lose other necessary things in the process. So, what is the best way to measure your progress? THE MIRROR! Seeing how your clothes fit, and how you feel. Maybe even have your fat tested (more on that later).

What's the last thing you might do on a diet? After about three weeks of all this starving, scale watching, agonizing, being frustrated, getting totally grouchy and tired (due to the lack of food) WE GIVE UP! Or try yet another one of those crazy diets. This is known as yo-yo dieting. Yo-yo dieting is going to stop NOW. YO-YO dieting is not only harmful to your body, but can put your metabolism so off kilter that it can make it extremely difficult for a person to lose weight, or even cause them NOT to be able to lose the weight. In this book you will learn how to eat properly, and maintain eating properly, so you will never have to diet again.

ATTITUDE

...is the most important part of life that either can make or break you. Attitude is everything! It also helps get everything that you desire in life. Attitude creates discipline, goals, enthusiasm, endurance and on and on and on. Once we achieve the attitude we need to succeed in anything we do, any goal can be obtainable within reason. This is true in weight management, work, daily life, even in stress - when things are at they're worst.

Positive thinking creates a positive attitude! Your attitude is more important than your aptitude. Attitude is going to make the New You succeed and continue to succeed.

85% of the reasons for successes, accomplishments, promotions, etc. are because of our attitudes, and only 15% because of our technical expertise (acquired facts). This means we spend 90% of our educational time and dollars developing that part which is responsible for only 15% of our success. Of course we need education in the technical term, but how much of your time is spent on the "thinking" aspect? For most of us, very little. When we do, where is it spent learning? You need to ask yourself this question.

Positive attitudes come from within, along with our surroundings. If you subject yourself to negative people, TV, reading and listening material, you will gradually become the same product in which you are surrounding yourself. Now you are saying, "No, not me! I can let it go in one ear and out the other." You may THINK you can, but on a subconscious level your brain is taking it in and processing it. Over time you will become accustomed to it, and don't even notice you've retained it. Take smoking for example (even if you don't smoke), when you take that first puff (or sniff) you cough and choke, and maybe sneeze. Your body is telling you to NOT put that into your body. But you continue and continue, and finally you're

3

smoking (or smelling) it with no problem.   Your body has gradually become accustomed to it.   The brain works in the same manner, only we are feeding it information. If you create a positive surrounding and eliminate as much negative as you can, you will change your attitude about life in general and become healthier along with creating a positive attitude.

WE CAN ALTER EATING HABITS BY ALTERING OUR ATTITUDE.

It took a continuous process of forcing myself to stop thinking of negatives.   When one entered my mind, I would stop myself and try to turn it around to think something positive. I even had to sit back and take a close look at my family and friends and decide which ones were healthy for me, and which ones were not.

Altering our attitude can give more confidence.

To my amazement, I could soon see which ones influenced me to be more self destructive just by how they viewed life in a negative manner. This is NOT an easy thing to do as it draws us out of our comfort zone. It's hard to let go of negative surroundings, but a negative attitude gets you NO WHERE on your path to a healthier you, and a positive attitude can take you EVERYWHERE.

Optimist or pessimist, which one are you? An optimist takes action and a pessimist takes a seat. A person who is doing his best and is making a contribution is optimistic and confident because he is personally working on the SOLUTION. A pessimist, on the other hand, is taking from society with no effort to contribute.

Is the glass half full or half empty? Is the weather partly cloudy or partly sunny? Get the idea? In the glass scenario, the optimist is putting water in the glass where the pessimist is taking water out of the glass. In order to obtain your weight management goals, you must become optimistic about what you are setting out to do. YOU WILL SUCCEED IN A HEALTHY LIFESTYLE.

Have you ever been asked something and responded with, "WELL, I TRIED," or "I'M TRYING?" Or how about, "I ALMOST DID IT." And the dreaded, "I CAN'T." TRY, ALMOST and CAN'T are three very EMPTY (negative) words. They have no meaning. It boils down to not having the positive attitude to accomplish what you had set out to achieve. I WILL SUCCEED!

When I began a martial arts class I was about 200 pounds and feeling very intimidated. The teacher explained and demonstrated a difficult roll, (like a cartwheel, only rolling over on your shoulders). When it was my turn, I told him **I'd try**. I was thinking I was too heavy to do this. I froze and fell on my face. When it was my turn again, I said "**I can't** do this." The teacher pulled me aside and scolded me by saying the word "CAN'T" is

NOT allowed in his classroom. He proceeded to tell me I CAN do anything I want if I set my mind to it. Well, to make a long story short, I kept falling on my face until I changed my attitude and began doing the roll. The first time was SO EXCITING as I accomplished it. Out of excitement I continued to practice the rolling technique every chance I got. The teacher approached me after awhile and asked me to demonstrate the rolling technique to the class. The purpose of this little story is to help you to understand the right mental attitude will help you accomplish any task, small or large.

Attitude before accomplishment, not accomplishment before attitude.

SELF IMAGE

*Visualizing
your goal
helps you achieve
your goal.*

When we think of ourselves, it's usually a different picture than what other people see us as physically. Most people when looking for a new weight management program have had, or still have, low self esteem. This is strongly influenced by our outside surroundings. The mind needs to be fed along with the body; the right positive information is necessary to change what outside pressures have created over the years. IT BEGINS WITH YOU. Attitude altering is going to be the most difficult mind work that you will do. It is the key to finding out what you want in life, work, accomplishments, losing weight, and a **SELF IMAGE**.

First, form a mental picture of what you wish to look like. Keep that mental picture in your mind repeating daily, like you are rehearsing for a play. Stand confident, **BELIEVE IN YOUR-SELF**, and carry that with you from everyday forward. When you want to reach for that donut or whatever, pop that mental picture of a New You in your mind, and ask yourself, "What I'm

7

eating, is it going to get me there?" That will usually stop you, or cause you to think twice about the action you are about to take. Your attitude towards yourself starts at the beginning, NOT when you achieve your goal. To achieve your goal, you need the right attitude, and in turn it will bring you positive self esteem.

YOU CAN ONLY SEE IN OTHERS WHAT IS INSIDE YOU.

For us women, many times the way we LOOK may create our attitude. If we get up in the morning, put on sloppy clothes, we may be comfortable, but most times if we go out and run into someone we know in the grocery store, or another place dressed this way, we feel uncomfortable, embarrassed or even feel bad about ourselves. All because of the way we look. If we put on a little make up, and something we have in our closet that's casual and nice, we begin to feel good about ourselves and our attitude follows. If you are overweight, you might like many of us, try to hide it with baggy clothes rather than trying to spruce yourself up. Even if it's adding just a pair of earrings, or a dab of eye make up, a new pair of pants, or a little accessory, it doesn't matter. It will help you create a more positive self image.

NO ONE CAN LOWER YOUR SELF ESTEEM WITHOUT YOUR PERMISSION.

Low self esteem mainly comes from outside yourself. Over time you begin to believe what ever people are telling you, and you begin to live your life as though the things they were telling you have come true. They have come true only because you didn't BELIEVE IN YOURSELF, or LOVE YOURSELF enough to stand up for what you believed in. What ever your case was, it doesn't matter now. It's in the past. We are living for today and the future, so NOW we have to build up our self esteem and show those people they were wrong. People, or outside pressures, may think they know you, but they don't. You know yourself better than anyone on this earth, and you are the one to take charge of what you want in your life now. This is going to be a day by day process. It will be difficult at times, but no one has the right to say anything bad about you without your permission.

Once you work on this day by day, everyday, you will begin to notice little changes in yourself. You may walk with a little more confidence, you may be a little more assertive, you may learn to say NO more often if you don't want to do something. People may be puzzled over what's different about you, because they're seeing a change in you. Take notice of any changes happening mentally or physically. Write them down or just give yourself a pat on the back, for even noticing.

THAT IS A STEP TOWARDS A
POSITIVE SELF IMAGE.

*Positive
thoughts
make
us
young.*

*Negative
thoughts
make
us
old.*

CONFIDENCE AND FEAR

These two almost go hand in hand if you dwell on the negative. Because we are thinking positive now, we are going to become more positive, fearless people. Fear is being afraid of the unknown! That is why many people are afraid of REJECTION. We don't know what the other person thinks of us or is going to say. Usually, if we approach that person or situation face to face we walk away thinking, "That wasn't so bad after all." How many times have you done this? A shy person is most likely insecure with him or herself, and where does this come from? FEAR and lack of self confidence. You need to look at it as not looking so terrible, but as a <u>challenge</u> to conquer your fears. As you meet those challenges the fewer fears you will have and the more confidence you will build. This will make it easier in facing the tough challenges and decisions you will need to make in the future. Fear of what you'll look like with a New You, or what people think or say, make this a POSITIVE CHANGE.

Creating a good positive attitude will eliminate fears, and cause your self confidence to sky rocket. Sometimes when we are becoming confident, and people are taking notice, they are beginning to pay attention to what we are doing and look like. Think positive, stand tall, and keep that momentum up, don't go back; go forward. Fear may want to creep back in, but don't budge.

Don't be afraid to try new things, you may just be surprised.

I never used to wear make-up and always wore T-shirts and jeans: Coming from a country background, I didn't like to wear anything else. One day I thought I'd learn how to apply make-up, and give it a whirl. I only put on a light application, and put on some nice clothes that day, and I couldn't count how many compliments I received. I felt real good inside, but I wasn't sure about the attention I was getting. The next time I did the same, only this time my posture was more straight. People continued to tell me I was looking good. I was still shy of all the compliments, but I was feeling better. People take notice! They may ask, "What are you doing this for" or "Do you have a new love in your life?" The simple answer to this is, "I'm doing it for myself." Most people don't believe in this statement, because they don't understand how to make THEMSELVES happy. Happiness comes from WITHIN YOURSELF AND NO WHERE ELSE. Happiness will create all the confidence in yourself to get what YOU want in life. This is especially true in weight management! Confidence in yourself will allow you to create the person YOU want to be, and make that goal possible. Your fears melt away.

One more little story to help you on your way... Most of us walk with our shoulders a little (or a lot) hunched over. This is because we lack the confidence in ourselves. One of the first things my body building trainer told me was, "You need to stand up straight." I thought I was! She showed me how to throw my shoulders back and chest out with confidence. It looked good on her but when I did it, I looked in the mirror and burst out laughing. She saw a confident looking person, I saw a lady trying to look like the whole Marine Corp. marching in step, chest totally projected. I thought people would laugh at me. I turned that fear around and thought positive, and walked into work with the confident walk I was taught. I'm not large busted, but changing my posture sure brought what I have more up right. I noticed everyone watching me. Remember, this is NOT overextending your chest, just enough to bring your shoulders back, to bring your arms to your sides. I began to notice everyone was taking glances at my chest (mostly the men of course). I panicked with fear and wanted to hunch back to my

11

old way, but I decided to stand strong. The day passed, and I felt good about myself. I kept a positive attitude, faced my fear and grew a little more confident. The point to this little story is, don't let the outside pressures of what other people think shake your confidence. Stand strong and believe in yourself, also what you are trying to accomplish.

It took years to become the person you are today, therefore confidence does not come over night! It takes time, and with a positive attitude, facing your fears one by one, daily your confidence will grow and grow and grow and grow and grow and grow.

Even the smallest creature can have
less fears when confidence is achieved.

HABITS_____

We will first look at habits themselves, then you will want to take a look at your life style and see what are your good and bad habits; which ones you'll want to keep and which ones you'll want to change.

Good habits are sort of like money: They are difficult to acquire but easy to live with once you acquire them. Bad habits on the other hand are EASY to acquire, but difficult to live with. When you choose a habit, you can also choose the end result. If envisioning the end result helps you rid the bad habit, then do so. Humans are very visual animals.

Habits form VERY SLOWLY. Remember the smoker discussed earlier in ATTITUDES! He choked at first, then gradually, cigarette by cigarette, he was able to smoke more and more. This is the same with overeating, alcohol, drugs, profanity, excessive shopping or keeping up with the Jones's. What ever habits you have acquired, ask yourself, "Are my habits healthy for me?" I have never met anyone that said when they were little they wanted to grow up to be obese, alcoholic, anorexic, a drug addict, etc. People with these problems started out thinking what they were doing wasn't habit forming and probably said, "I can quit anytime", but before they knew it the habit had a hold on them and they were in deeper than they ever thought they'd be. The person justifies his habit in his mind, and continues to keep doing what he is doing. To realize his habit as a DESTRUCTIVE HABIT, and deciding to end it, is the first important decision. It takes discipline, determination, and the desire to become healthy again. All bad habits start slowly, maybe even from our childhood.

Habits took time to form, therefore, it will take time to end them. YOU CAN'T CHANGE A HABIT OVER NIGHT. Be patient with yourself and take it DAY BY DAY. Each day pat yourself on the back when you've succeeded that day with not falling back on the old bad habit. The end results are rewarding.

FRIEND'S HABITS STEADILY BECOME OUR HABITS.

NO ONE benefits from bad habits. People these days believe a little of something is harmless but in actuality, that LITTLE BIT starts the habits and trends of the future. Years ago on T. V. and in the theaters, you would rarely, if ever, hear a swear word, or see a shot of nudity. One movie did it and thought it harmless, then gradually it became more and more common. Look at the media today, at topics, profanity, and some borderline pornography. Now are you getting the picture how habits are formed?

Let's take a look at FOOD as a habit. As a child, what kind of habits did your parents instill at the table? Were you able to walk away with some food left on your plate? Or were your parents like mine always saying, "Clean your plate and you can

leave the table," or "I don't want any left-overs for tomorrow, so eat up." Or another famous one is, "Eat your food, there are starving children all over this world." Does this sound familiar?

Don't just
YAK about it,
DO IT!

Maybe you started your eating habits by filling in the void of other emotions that you needed, but weren't receiving. Either way, you developed habits slowly.

Emotions can control our habits in a big way. While attending a nutrition class on the subject of eating habits the instructor asked us to examine our eating habits by writing them on a piece of paper. She then asked us, "How many of you go to work, or go out, then come home, and the first thing you do is open the refrigerator?" I thought at first, "Not me", but when I began to look closely at my habits, I noticed I did this every time I came home. It astounded me! I was eating for comfort.

Before we head into how we can eliminate bad habits I want you to ponder the thought that habits are like attitudes. We acquire different attitudes from the people we associate with. Habits are also formed by the people we associate with. If we associate with people that have bad habits, we become immune and desensitized to them and STEADILY, THEIR HABITS BECOME OURS. This includes our eating habits.

I want to share with you a situation that I hope you can remember, look back on and help you eliminate your bad habits.

My younger brother was a recovering alcoholic and drug addict. He lived in Florida. He began his habits slowly at the age of about thirteen, going through life until age 25 with destructive habits. One Christmas eve he decided to end his destructive life and checked himself into a detoxification center. With a year of struggling and fighting his habits, getting into a halfway house, then to a 3/4 house, at last he was clean. These weren't easy habits to break. With determination, desire, self confidence and support from friends, he made it and turned his life around completely. Our family knew all about destructive habits, and knew underneath he was a good-hearted person screaming to get out. Underneath he was the most loving, helping person that anyone could know. People were coming out of the walls that knew him, and they all had some kind of good little story of what he had done, something good for each and every one of them. The outcome of him breaking his habits was nothing but good. The point to this story is: YOU GET NOTHING OUT OF BAD HABITS, AND ALL GOOD FROM GOOD HABITS.

We are like a rope. We will weave a thread each day until the rope becomes so big and strong, it will be too strong to break. If you are a weak rope, add threads (healthy habits) to make your rope stronger.

Use your new positive attitude and self confidence to throw the bad habits out of the saddle and put the new ones on top of the horse.

Now that we've talked about what habits can do to a person, we want to get rid of the old bad habits.

Healthy habits
come from
healthy thoughts.

BOOTING THE HABIT

The first thing that must be done is to <u>clear our minds, bodies and souls</u>. Cut off any bad habits before they get a chance to start. If you haven't begun a bad habit, why start now? Your instincts will tell you if it's wrong. Listen to your instincts! If it feels wrong, DON'T DO IT! We have enough to contend with in our lives, than to add more stress.

The second thing is to <u>avoid bad habits, if you are tempted by them</u>. Temptations are going to always be offered to you. It's up to you now to make the right choice. With the New You, build the rope stronger, say no thank you and walk away. You will feel WONDERFUL for doing this healthy thing for yourself.

The last thing is to <u>set a good example for someone else</u>. By doing so, you are not only creating a healthy lifestyle for you, but maybe someone else who looks up to you. (children, a co-worker, a friend, a family member). People will want to follow your example.

DON'T TRY TO CONQUER MORE THAN ONE BAD HABIT AT A TIME.

You have to be the one to quit the bad habit, NOT SOMEONE ELSE! So many times we do things for other people, for various reasons, but it's the wrong reason. We are becoming healthy now, therefore we are learning to TAKE CARE OF OURSELVES. Many times we lose weight not for ourselves, but because we are looking for acceptance, attention, or just plain love. We think if we shed those pounds, these things will come to us from someone else. If you look deep at why you do anything, it should be because you are doing it for YOURSELF. It's time to take control of your life. Take your horse by the reins and lead him to a healthy path, not to the cliff where he may fall and self-destruct.

One of the things that greatly helped me as I worked on breaking my bad habits, was to talk and listen to people that have succeeded. My bad habit is overeating, therefore, I listened to people who lost weight and KEPT it off. I heard how good they felt, how much more energy they had and their struggle to get there. It will surprise you to how much motivation this will give you to keep you going. When I met my second Professional Trainer, I was so excited to hit a new level and keep me motivated, as I didn't want to go back to my old habits. If you don't have anyone to talk to, write to someone, or do something that will help keep you motivated and walking down the right path.

You will be taking away one bad habit at a time. Don't try to conquer any more than one at a time, as it will be too much for

you. When you take one habit away, sub-consciously another wants to take it's place. You will need to be COMPLETELY AWARE of yourself during this time. Try to fill this void with a healthy activity of some kind. If you notice a NEW bad habit forming, STOP IT NOW. This is why we only do one habit at a time. Remember, <u>a habit is all in your mind</u>, like an attitude.

*"Watch out partner,
I'm gonna bury
that bad habit".*

You'll need to keep your mind filled and fed with confidence and inspirational thoughts, and continue to tell yourself, "I CAN DO THIS. I CAN BEAT THIS." No one can help you but you. If you've got your hand on the refrigerator door, or even the cupboard door for that matter, STOP and ask yourself WHY? If it's because you're bored, lonely, angry or frustrated, your bad habit is still trying to convince you to go back. If it's because you are HUNGRY, then go ahead, open the door. Think about everything you do and ask yourself why, analyze it, and make the choice to continue or stop.

Again, visualize yourself as the end product of kicking this bad habit. Visualize it day in, day out. Minute by minute, second by second. The more you visualize it, the more you will help it to come about. Be optimistic about this end result. Old habits and negative thoughts WILL try to creep back in. Take that thought by the horns and throw it right out of the corral. We don't need those old ways any longer.

Just for a split second, look back on your past (we normally won't go back as we always want to move forward), and see if your habits enhanced your life or hurt your life. If the habits hindered your life, in your quest forward to a productive, happy, healthy way of life, then you will have less work on yourself to do. Beware you are always susceptible to a bad habit. Habits will never be eliminated 100%. You will have to make the decision daily, to go back or move forward. I know you want to move forward.

In brief, habits can be broken, just like a wild horse can be broken. Take each one slowly, as they were developed slowly. Give yourself encouragement, and praise yourself daily. Don't be tempted by all the people out there who want to see you fail and fall back. Sit strong in the saddle and don't budge or walk away. This will get you to the new life you want. You are on your way and those people who are trying to bring you back to your old ways, may change too and may just follow you.

SECTION II: RECIPES FOR THE HEART
DYNAMICS OF HEALTHY EATING

SITTING ON THE HORSE

Dynamics of Healthy Eating

UNDERSTANDING NUTRITION LABELS___

With the new nutrition labels on packaging it is much easier to figure the nutrition value of what we are eating. Later in this section there is an example of nutrition labels.

The old labels had to be calculated from grams to calories. If you didn't know how to calculate it, most likely you gave up or bought a product anyway. The labels now are much simpler to read. Besides reading the nutrition facts one must read the list of ingredients. It is very surprising what can be hidden in the labels. You may think reading labels is going to take too much time. In the beginning it may take an effort, but you will be amazed at how quickly you retain this information and gradually, will know approximately how much junk is put into packaged foods. Hidden factors such as sugars, fats, and sodium are the key items to look for. Sugar comes in various forms, such as Fructose, Sucrose and Dextrose. If you must have sugar, the best kind is Fructose (comes from fruit). Sugars can be hidden as Fructose, Sucrose and Dextrose.

When trying to lower weight, it's best to stay away from sugar, as sugar stimulates insulin levels and activates enzymes in the stomach lining, which promotes fat storage.

OILS are another item to watch closely. There are so many kinds of fats, but the simple thing to remember about fats is to avoid Saturated Fat, or those coming from animal, dairy, and three oils of the vegetable group which are coconut, palm and palm kernel. These should be avoided! <u>Saturated fats work against lowering your cholesterol</u>.

Finally, **SODIUM**. Most people forget to watch this very important factor. Sodium creates water retention. Our diet NEEDS sodium, but because it's in our daily foods, we can omit added salt to our diets. We only need 2000 grams of salt for a whole day, so watch those labels. Salt also is taxing on our kidneys, and on our heart. SERVING SIZES on the labels can fool you too. When reading the calories and fats, be sure you look at the serving size. This can be deceiving if you look at calories and fat and not the serving size. Our example label shows 1 serving size is approximately 1 cup. BE AWARE when figuring your own nutrition plan. Don't be fooled by labels saying they are cholesterol free, fat free, or sugar free. Remember those hidden items? When reading the ingredient portion, keep in mind the first ingredient listed happens to be what the product is primarily made of. Looking at our example label, whole oat flour is listed first, therefore that product consists mostly of whole oat flour. Read the ingredients, and you'll be amazed.

"Ability is Important, dependability is Critical."

DISSECTING THE LABEL_____

Nutrition Facts
Serving Size 2 Pieces (88g) • Servings Per Container 4

	Amount Per Serv.	% DV*	Amount Per Piece	% DV*
Calories	260		130	
Calories From Fat	35		20	
Total Fat	3.5g	6%	2g	3%
Saturated Fat	1.5g	4%	1g	2%
Polyunsaturated	1g		.5g	
Monounsaturated	1g		.5g	
Cholesterol	0mg	0%	0mg	0%
Sodium	228mg	13%	114mg	8%
Total Carbohydrates	50g	23%	25g	12%
Dietary Fiber	4g	6%	2g	3%
Sugars	28g		14g	
Protein	8g		4g	

Vitamin A	0%	0%
Vitamin C	0%	0%
Calcium	4%	2%
Iron	12 %	6%
Thiamin	2%	**
Riboflavin	6%	3%
Niacin	2%	**

*Percent Daily Values are based ona 2,000 calorie diet. Your daily values may be higher or lower depending on your calorie needs.
**Contains less than 2 % of the Reference Daily Intake for these nutrients.

Calories per gram:
Fat 12 • Carbohydrate 8 • Protein 6

INGREDIENTS: WHOLE WHEAT FLOUR, WHEAT STARCH, SUGAR, SALT, ENRICHED BLEACHED FLOUR (WHEAT FLOUR, NIACIN, REDUCED IRON, THIAMINE MONOMITRATE, RIBOFLAVIN), SPICES, LEAVENING (SODIUM BICARBONATE, SODIUM ALUMINUM PHOSPHATE, MONOCALCIUM PHOSPHATE), SOY FLOUR, WHEY, EGG WHITES, GUAR GUM.

SERVING SIZE: How to measure 1 full serving.

SERVING SIZE PER CONTAINER: Tells you how many servings the product has inside the package.

CALORIES: Depicts the total calories for 1 full serving. If there happens to be two columns, most likely the second column is with an added product, such as; with 1/2 cup skim milk. Calories in the second column will be the total with 1/2 cup of skim milk.

TOTAL FAT: Next to these words will be the gram quantity. Grams will be put next to each item after this point, in case you want to calculate it yourself. Next, the percentage per serving will be given.

Below the Total Fat portion, the fats will be broken down further to show the percentage of each fat: Saturated fat, polyunsaturated fat and monounsaturated fat.

CHOLESTEROL, SODIUM, POTASSIUM: Follow in the same manner as Total Fat.

25

CHOLESTEROL, SODIUM, POTASSIUM: Follow in the same manner as Total Fat.

CARBOHYDRATES: Show the total per serving. Next, it will be broken down just like the fat portion: Dietary fiber, sugars and other carbohydrates.

PROTEIN: Is the last item on the top portion of the Nutrition Facts. This sometimes will only give the grams. This is usually due to the small amount of protein in the product.

VITAMIN PORTION: This section will list all the vitamins and minerals the product has, along with the percentages per serving. As a beginner you do not need to worry about this portion, unless you are under a doctor's care and are on a special diet.

PERCENT DAILY VALUES: This is a rounded amount of calorie consumption the RDA has chosen. It is based on a persons calorie intake being 2000 calories. So if your daily calorie intake is lower/higher, the percentages will change slightly.

Next a breakdown of Fat, Cholesterol, Sodium, Potassium, and Total Carbohydrates will be given.

INGREDIENTS: Ingredients are listed in the order of items that are found in the product. They are listed in sequence where the first item is found the most, and the last item is found the least in the product. (Example: If sugar is the first item listed, the product is mostly sugar).

VITAMINS AND MINERALS: Even though these are listed above, these are also broken down further into their scientific names.

Remember when reading labels, the three most important factors to watch for are FAT, SUGARS, and SODIUM. And remember to note the serving size.

*A SHOPPING HINT: When shopping, try to shop the outer circle of the grocery store. This is where the fresh foods, and the daily food groups you need are located. Anything in the center is processed. Look at your grocery store the next time you go.

Nutrition Facts

Serving Size 18 Pieces (124g)
Servings Per Container 4

	Amount Per Serv.	% DV*
	340	
Calories	18	
Calories From Fat	1.5g	3%
Total Fat	.5mg	1%
Cholesterol	134mg	9%
Sodium		
Total Carbohydrates	64g	28%
Dietary Fiber	2g	6%
Sugars	18g	
Protein	1g	

	0%
Vitamin A	0%
Vitamin C	4%
Calcium	12%
Iron	2%
Thiamin	6%
Riboflavin	2%
Niacin	

*Percent Daily Values are based on a 2,000 calorie diet. Your daily values may be higher or lower depending on your calorie needs.
**Contains less than 2 % of the Reference Daily Intake for these nutrients.

Calories per gram:

Fat 12 • Carbohydrate 8 • Protein 6

INGREDIENTS: WHOLE WHEAT FLOUR, WHEAT STARCH, SUGAR, SALT, ENRICHED BLEACHED FLOUR (WHEAT FLOUR, NIACIN, REDUCED IRON, THIAMINE MONONITRATE, RIBOFLAVIN), SPICES, LEAVENING (SODIUM BICARBONATE, SODIUM ALUMINUM PHOSPHATE, MONOCALCIUM PHOSPHATE), SOY FLOUR, WHEY, EGG WHITES, GUAR GUM.

5 Calories
No Fat • No Cholesterol

Nutrition Facts

Serving Size 1/2 Cup (128g)
Servings Per Container: 4

Amount Per Serving

		From Fat 130
Calories 250		
	3.5g	6%
Total Fat	1.5g	4%
Saturated Fat	1g	
Polyunsaturated	1g	
Monounsaturated	0mg	0%
Cholesterol	228mg	13%
Sodium		
Total	4g	6%
Dietary Fiber	28g	
Sugars	8g	
Protein		

Vitamin A	4%	Calcium	24%
Vitamin C	2%	Iron	8%

*Percents (%) of a Daily Value is based on a 2,000 calorie diet. Your Daily Value may be higher or lower depending on your calorie needs.

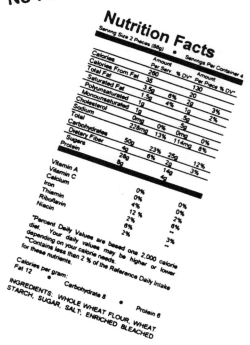

Nutrition Facts

Serving Size 2 Pieces (88g) • Servings Per Container 4

	Amount Per Serv.	% DV*	Amount Per Piece	% DV*
Calories	260		130	
Calories From Fat	35		20	
Total Fat	3.5g	6%	2g	3%
Saturated Fat	1.5g	4%	1g	
Polyunsaturated	1g		.5g	2%
Monounsaturated	1g		.5g	
Cholesterol	0mg	0%	0mg	0%
Sodium	228mg	13%	114mg	
Total Carbohydrates	50g	23%	25g	8%
Dietary Fiber	4g	6%	2g	12%
Sugars	28g		14g	3%
Protein	8g		4g	

Vitamin A	0%	
Vitamin C	0%	
Calcium	4%	0%
Iron	12 %	2%
Thiamin	2%	6%
Riboflavin	6%	
Niacin	2%	3%

*Percent Daily Values are based on a 2,000 calorie diet. Your daily values may be higher or lower depending on your calorie needs.
**Contains less than 2 % of the Reference Daily Intake for these nutrients.

Calories per gram:
Fat 12 • Carbohydrate 8 • Protein 6

INGREDIENTS: WHOLE WHEAT FLOUR, WHEAT STARCH, SUGAR, SALT, ENRICHED BLEACHED

ALL NATURAL

28

CARBOHYDRATES

Carbohydrates are where we get most of our energy from out of the three categories (proteins, carbohydrates, and fats). So it's important to get the proper amount of Carbohydrates to give us the fuel and energy we need to get through the day.

Don't get confused, but Carbohydrates are sugars. There are many forms of sugars, and they come in a variety of chains. This is all known to a biochemist as saccharides. We won't go into detail on this now. All I want you to remember is the two kinds for now. SIMPLE carbohydrates, and COMPLEX carbohydrates. The simplest way to remember these is "Simple" is all fruit and vegetables. "Complex" are starchy carbohydrates like pasta's, rice, potatoes and breads.

The body sends the modified carbohydrates into the bloodstream then to the liver and muscles as energy. This is where you might hear the term glycogen. Glycogen (carbohydrates) are stored energy. If there isn't enough glycogen stored and a person doesn't eat enough carbohydrates, the body will become fatigued, and will have little or no energy.

Doing exercises will quickly deplete the glycogen storage. Anerobics will deplete them faster than Aerobics. Why? When Doing Anerobics, the exercises ask for a much harder quicker result in energy, so the energy is pulled from the muscle tissue much more rapidly. Aerobics is a longer, more endurance exercise, and glycogen can be released much more slowly.

If too many carbohydrates are being eaten and a person is not exercising, the glycogen will be stored, but when it begins to overflow because the storage is full, it will begin to be stored as fat.

Because carbohydrates are in the sugar family, they play a part in also your insulin levels. Have you ever heard the saying,

"My blood sugar is low?" or noticed a person tends to be grouchy that hasn't eaten, but after they eat something, a few minutes later, they're fine again? This is because their storage has been depleted, then re-boosted. When hungry and good food (carbohydrates) are eaten the body will respond in a healthy, more stabilized manner. But if for example a candy bar is eaten, because it's all sugar, it will send the body's insulin level really high, and you'll feel great for a short time, then fatigued when it is gone. There will be more on this in the Meal Timing section of this book.

Stable blood sugar will promote a better glycogen storage. So we want to keep a steady intake of complex carbohydrates, so our blood sugar levels don't go on a roller coaster ride. This will help take away your hunger cravings, too. Being consistent is the key with carbohydrates.

EXAMPLES OF CARBOHYDRATES:

Beans
  Lentils
  Lima beans
Breads
  Bagels
  Bulgar
  Buns (hot dog and
      hamburger)
  Corn bread
  French
  Muffins (English &
  low fat)
  Pumpernickel
  Raisin
  Rolls
  Rye
  White
  Whole Wheat
Cereal
  Bran cereals

Bran flakes
Grapenuts
Granola
Oatmeal
Shredded wheat
Wheat Germ
Crackers
Pasta
  Angel Hair
  Macaroni
  Shells
  Spaghetti
  Vegetable
Rice (white and brown)
Tortillas
Yams and Sweet Potatoes
Vegetables
  Alfalfa Sprouts
  Asparagus
  Artichokes

Bamboo Shoots	Eggplant
Beans, String	Lettuce
Beets	Mushrooms
Bok Choy	Onions
Broccoli	Parsnips
Brussel Sprouts	Peas
Cabbage	Peppers (red, green
Carrots	and yellow)
Cauliflower	Potatoes
Celery	Spinach
Corn	Squash
Cucumber	Tomatoes

"Being good for yourself is doing something nice for someone else."

PROTEINS

Proteins are essential for muscle tissue growth and recuperation. Your body needs approximately 0.5 - 1.0 grams of protein per pound of LEAN body mass. Too much protein in the diet can cause weight gain along with elevated cholesterol. How much protein do YOU need is going to depend on your activity (aerobic exercise) level and other factors. For example, let's use a person with a weight of 150 pounds. **The LEAN body mass* for this weight is approximately 120 pounds.** To get this figure multiply **120 pounds x 1.0 = 120 grams of protein. Take 120 grams X 4** (remember, there are 4 calories to every gram of protein), and that equals **480 calories of protein.**

Persons weight	150 Pounds
Lean body mass	120 Pounds
1.0 gram of protein	X 1.0
Grams of protein	120
4 calories per gram	X 4
Calories of protein	480

That's how much protein this person will need for the day. Now if he is very active, he may need much more. If this person is inactive he may need less. We will go into this with more detail later. Exercise plays an important role in how much food intake you will need. Exercise regulates how many carbohydrates, protein and fat we can have on a daily basis.

Good sources of protein are from egg whites, turkey, chicken (skinned white meat), fish and beans. What happened to pork and beef, you ask? Pork has too much fat, and there are very few types of beef that are lean enough. If you decide to stick with only beef because you are a beef lover, then it's important to buy the leanest beef you can find, such as beef flank steak.

My recipes don't have many beef ingredients. Other meats can be put in it's place. Being a beef lover myself and <u>slowly</u> substituting other meats in place of beef, now I don't miss it much. When I do eat beef, it's in moderation and the leanest I can get. But once a week is O.K. Watch the meat proportions, as they can fool you. Your results will be <u>much slower</u>, also, if you incorporate beef too often in your diet.

*Lean Body Mass: Body weight minus body fat; composed primarily of muscle, bone and other nonfat tissue (Can be found through a fat testing device).

EXAMPLES OF PROTEINS:

FISH AND SHELLFISH
- Bass
- Bluefish
- Catfish
- Cod
- Clams
- Crayfish
- Crab
- Haddock
- Halibut
- Lobster
- Octopus
- Oysters
- Perch
- Pollack
- Salmon
- Scallops
- Shrimp
- Sole
- Squid
- Swordfish
- Trout
- Tuna

POULTRY
- Chicken
- Cornish Hens
- Turkey

OTHER
- Beans
- Beef
- Pork
- Eggs
- Lamb
- Lentils
- Liver
- Tofu

UNDERSTANDING FAT

One of the most mis-understood part of a healthy diet is FAT, but it is an important factor to our diet. If a person sticks to the basics of sitting in the saddle, rather than trying to under-stand the scientific aspect of fat, a person can grasp the idea and carry it with them from day to day. **Yes, we want to reduce fat** in the diet, but NO we don't want to cut it out completely. Your body requires a certain amount of fat to function (depending on your body, approximately 15 - 25 %). Without ANY fat in our diet our bodies couldn't function their best. There will most likely, be fat in anything that you eat whether it is hidden or easy to see in the labels, just like sodium. Even if the label reads 0% fat you can be guaranteed that there is still a little fat in that product. It may just be an under the regulated amount to quote it as "No Fat" or even "Low Fat". This is where label reading becomes very important. Just remember, FAT EATEN IS FAT GAINED! Let's look at a nutrition label.

Nutrition Facts

Serving Size 2 Pieces (88g) Servings Per Container 4

	Amount Per Serv	% DV*
Calories	260	
Calories From Fat	35	
Total Fat	3.5g	6%
Saturated Fat	1.5g	4%
Polyunsaturated	1g	
Monounsaturated	1g	
Cholesterol	0mg	0%
Sodium	228mg	13%
Total Carbohydrates	50g	23%
Dietary Fiber	4g	6%
Sugars	28g	
Protein	8g	

The average person only needs about 15 - 25% fat in their daily diet, so if we look at the 15%, we see this label has 3% fat in each serving. So, if one serving is consumed there is still 12% of the daily intake left for the rest of the day. Yes, you will need to keep track of your daily consumption in the beginning. But after you become used to the saddle and the way it feels, you will gradually know how much fat is in each food. If you are looking at the old label, the only the only thing to remember is 1 GRAM OF FAT = 9 CALORIES (or you can round it to 10 if this easier for you to remember). KEEP IT SIMPLE!

One gram of fat = 9 calories.

For those of you who are watching cholesterol levels, when reading nutrition labels you need to watch for mono- or polyunsaturated fats over saturated fats. Saturated fats are the fats which clog our system. When buying products with fats in them stay clear of hydrogenated vegetable oil, coconut oil, palm oil, cocoa butter and palm kernel. These are saturated fats.

Let's take a closer look at the fat section of the label:

When looking at the fat section in detail, don't let it confuse you. The first line is the total amount of fat <u>per serving</u> (2.5 or 4%). Next is the breakdown of different fats for you:

Saturated fat	= 1.5 g. or 3 % of the Recommended Daily Allowance (RDA)
Polyunsaturated	= 1 g.
Monounsaturated	= 1 g.
Total	3.5 grams

Saturated fat makes up most of the fat in this product, and because we want to eliminate as much SATURATED FAT as possible from our diet, do we want this product? NO!

EXAMPLES OF FAT:

Butter
Cheese
     Cheddar
     Cream Cheese
     Jack
     Mozzarella
Dressing
     1000 Island
     Blue Cheese
     French
     Italian
     Ranch
Margarine
Mayonnaise
Sandwich Spreads

Nuts
     Cashews
     Filberts
     Peanuts
     Macadamia
Oils
     Canola
     Corn
     Olive
     Peanut
     Safflower
     Sesame
     Vegetable
Milk Products
     Sour Cream
     Half and half
     Buttermilk
     Whole milk
     Creams

"Start simple and build up. To build up is to build confidence."

FAT SUBSTITUTIONS

Now you are saying, "Wait a minute; NO FAT, NO FLAVOR", right? WRONG!!! The more the public becomes health conscious, the more demand there is for manufacturers to develop substitutes for fat and sugar (we'll get into sugar later). Go to your spice section and look at all the options you have. Some cookbooks will specify one low fat product and you'll find it in all their recipes. Everyone cooks different and has different taste buds; therefore, the recipes in this book will give you a guideline, but you will be able to substitute an alternative if you don't like the choices given. The guidelines are here, but they're for you to experiment with. Just remember when modifying to use the lowest fat, and monounsaturated fat is best.

Some examples of fat substitutions are:

- Low fat cooking spray.

- Substitute Butters, such as Molly McButter, Butter Buds (both dry and liquid) or Wonderslim.

- Applesauce, prunes (baby) or Wonderslim can replace oils in cooking.

Check the substitution section for fat alternative options.

UNDERSTANDING SUGAR

Sugar is an additive, plain and simple. It is usually a REFINED sugar, but it has many names. Watch your labels again for names like sucrose, invert sugar, corn sugar, corn syrups and solids, high-fructose corn syrup and honey. Even though the label may say NO SUGAR ADDED, read the ingredients. The reason for staying away from sugar when trying to control one's eating habits is, because an excess amount of sugar can upset the metabolic balance, especially in a hypoglycemic or diabetic person. Sugar is known to the diet world as EMPTY calories, which means it has NO NUTRITIONAL VALUE.

Sugars, believe it or not, come from the carbohydrate family, which come in forms of simple or complex carbohydrates. We will not get into this, but it is important to know that sugar is added to the carbohydrate list. Sugar is digested quickly from the mouth to the bloodstream which causes the quick exertion of energy followed by a drop in energy (fatigue).

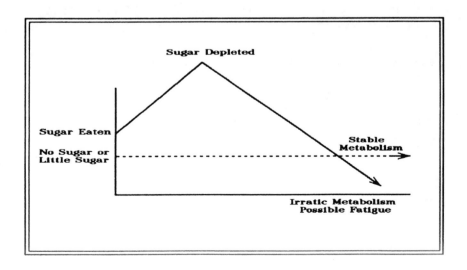

When sugar is ingested it brings your blood sugar levels to an extremely high point very fast, and when the sugar is depleted the blood sugar level drops dramatically and hits bottom, which then causes a tired sensation. This is NOT what a person is trying to achieve when they are trying to control eating habits. We want to establish a even metabolism through out the day so our bodies can work at their optimum level. This is what keeps us in balance, therefore healthy.

Now you are able to understand the basics of sugar, and it's importance to the metabolism.

NATURAL SUGAR SUBSTITUTES_____

Fruits also provide sugar and can be used by people with diabetes in cooking . They provide the same dose as sugar or honey but are more valuable nutritionally. Fruits enter the body as sugar diluted in large amounts of water and can mix with vitamins and minerals. Remember, we're trying to balance the metabolism and sugar brings this out of balance. Fruits should be treated as sugar when eaten, as they raise the blood sugar just as refined sugar does.

Fruit juices can also be substituted for many things, as you will see in the recipe section of this book. Remember, natural is the best, and we want to obtain as much nutritional value as possible. Applesauce is very popular for baking, too.

What about Honey? Honey is a natural SUGAR. Honey does contains a few vitamins and minerals, but not very many. They all break down to being a sugar.

"All that sugar made me sleepy."

*ARTIFICIAL SUGAR SUBSTITUTES*_____

Because of people's common concern about cutting back on sugar intake, manufacturers have developed alternatives. There are many out there but the three most known to us are EQUAL, NUTRA SWEET, and SWEET 'N LOW. SWEET 'N LOW can be used either cold or hot (in cooking) since it does not contain aspartame, which looses it's sweetness with excessive heat.

To convert Sweet 'N Low to Sugar: It takes three packets of Sweet 'N Low to make one teaspoon sugar:

1 tsp. Sweet 'N Low	= 3 pkts. = 1/4 C. Sugar
1 1/4 tsp. Sweet 'N Low	= 4 pkts. = 1/3 C. Sugar
2 tsp. Sweet 'N Low	= 6 pkts. = 1/2 C. Sugar
3 tsp. Sweet 'N Low	= 9 pkts. = 3/4 C. Sugar
4 tsp. Sweet 'N Low	= 12 pkts. = 1 C. Sugar

Equal and Nutrasweet can also be used as the same amounts of Sweet 'N Low.

THE WATERING TROUGH_____

Water is a necessary nutrient to our daily diet. Without it, we would die. Humans can only survive a short time without it, but food we can survive weeks without. Unfortunately, most of us don't drink enough of water. Here's just a few of many things water does for our bodies:

- Flushes waste products throughout the body

- Carries nutrients through the body

- Is a lubricant around the joints

- Participates in chemical reactions in the body

- Helps regulate the body's temperature

- Is a shock absorber inside the spinal cord, eyes, and other areas.

The list goes on and on. So, you can see some of the importance that water has in making our bodies function properly.

"How much water should I drink," you ask? There is no exact amount, due to each person's different body chemistry. How much energy is expended in the day differs with each person. A guideline for adults is at least six to eight, eight ounce glasses of water per day. If exercising, a person expends 1.0 to 1.5 gallons.

*NOTE: 1/2 cup per 100 calories expended.

Not enough water can cause DEHYDRATION. This occurs when the output of water exceeds the input. For example, exercising without drinking water during exercise can cause weakness, a rapid thirst, and exhaustion. In extreme cases, dehydration can cause confusion, convulsions, and in severve cases, even death.

Is there such a thing as TOO MUCH water? It is difficult, but possible to do. This is called WATER INTOXICATION. It occurs if water content in the body becomes too high, and can cause kidney disorders that reduce the urine output. In extreme cases, this condition can also cause confusion, convulsions, and death.

You might think you only need to drink water when you are thirsty. WRONG! Thirst is NOT a good indicator that your body needs water. By the time the thirst mechanism clicks in, inside your brain, the body is already deprived of its water supply. If you take the time to drink when you get thirsty, it still does not replenish the water supply already lost. To keep the body replenished, continuous water through the day is best.

So, now you tell me, "But I drink a lot of coffee, tea, and Cola's, and they have water in them." Yes, they do, but things **made with** water can be counter productive. Water means WATER.

We need water to flush, transport and provide all the nutrients our body needs. I can't express how important water is to weight loss and gain. I didn't believe it myself until my body began to change, and now I think I have a water bottle permanently growing from my hand.

Bottled waters sometimes are stripped of the nutrients we get in our water supply. Be aware that tap water and bottled water are not the same. Tap water has chemicals added to make it drinkable. Artesian water contains <u>some nutrients</u>, and bottled water has very little to none.

Either way, **DRINK ENOUGH WATER.**

CALORIC INTAKE

Americans that have dieted off and on for years, known as yo-yo dieters, are looking to lose weight quick and easy. This is the wrong concept, and more times than not, those dieters have probably put the weight back on, and then some. Diets are a quick fix, but they are not permanent. Eating a healthy, well balanced plan will cause you to lose weight at a slower pace, but it will stay off longer, if not permanently (permanently will depend on you). Once your weight is where you are comfortable with it, it then must be maintained or it will come back. Most people will reach that comfortable weight, then think, "I did it," and go out and splurge. Old habits begin to come back and before they know it the weight is back. On the average, a person should not try to lose more than one to two pounds a week. One pound of body fat stores about 3,500 calories. A person must add or subtract 500 calories a day to either gain or lose weight, when trying to gain or lose a pound or two a week. This also helps to keep the body in balance while weight is being gained or lost at a slow pace. So, let's do some calculating.

First, we'll get rid of the concept of THREE SQUARE MEALS a day. To keep the body's metabolism stable, a person needs to keep it fueled, requiring a person to eat more frequently, eating 3 - 6 small meals a day (4 - 6 is great), and in smaller proportions. Next, we'll concentrate on learning what to put on our plates and how much. Carbohydrates, protein, and fat are going to be our main concern as beginners.

To figure how many calories you should be taking in daily for weight loss, you can eat 10 CALORIES PER POUND OF BODY WEIGHT. See the calorie charts for women and men later in this section. Example: A 150 pound woman can eat 10 calories per pound of body weight, equaling 1,500 calories per day:

Weight	150 Pounds
Calories	X 10 Per Pound
	1,500 Total Calories

It's that simple. More calories may be needed depending on your exercise expenditure and other physical needs, such as pregnancy, nursing or other medical reasons. We will talk about this later. Figure approximately 55% carbohydrates, 30% protein and 15% fat. Imagine a plate in front of you, and placing about two-thirds carbohydrates on it, such as rice, and the other one-third protein, such as chicken. This is a basic idea you can keep in mind. Now, let's break it down even further.

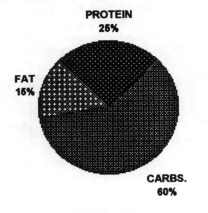

PROTEIN
25%

FAT
15%

CARBS.
60%

Remember:

1 gram carbohydrate = 4 calories
1 gram protein = 4 calories
1 gram fat = 9 calories

CALORIE CHART FOR WOMEN

WEIGHT LOSS
Calories allowed per day

LBS	Hours of exercise 0	1	2	3
90	1000	1000	1760	2240
95	1000	1000	1860	2340
100	1000	1000	1960	2440
105	1000	1055	2060	2540
110	1000	1130	2160	2640
115	1000	1205	2260	2740
120	1000	1280	2360	2840
125	1000	1355	2460	2940
130	1000	1430	2560	3040
135	1000	1505	2660	3140
140	1000	1580	2760	3240
145	1000	1655	2860	3340
150	1000	1730	2960	3440
155	1015	1805	3060	3540
160	1080	1880	3160	3640
165	1145	1955	3260	3740
170	1210	2030	3360	3840
175	1275	2105	3460	3940
180	1340	2180	3560	4040
185	1405	2255	3660	4140
190	1470	2330	3760	4240
195	1535	2405	3860	4340
200	1600	2480	3960	4440
205	1665	2555	4060	4540
210	1730	2630	4160	4640
215	1795	2705	4260	4740
220	1860	2780	4360	4840
225	1925	2855	4460	4940
230	1990	2930	4560	5040
235	2055	3005	4660	5140
240	2120	3080	4760	5240
245	2185	3155	4860	5340
250	2250	3230	4960	5440
255	2315	3305	5060	5540
260	2380	3380	5160	5640
265	2445	3455	5260	5740
270	2510	3530	5360	5840
275	2575	3605	5460	5940
280	2640	3680	5560	6040
285	2705	3755	5660	6140
290	2770	3830	5760	6240
295	2835	3905	5860	6340
300	2900	3980	5960	6440

WEIGHT GAIN
Calories allowed per day

LBS	Hours of exercise 0	1	2	3
70	1735	2355	3185	3665
75	1800	2430	3285	3765
80	1865	2505	3385	3865
85	1930	2580	3485	3965
90	1995	2655	3585	4065
95	2060	2730	3685	4165
100	2125	2805	3785	4265
105	2190	2880	3885	4365
110	2255	2955	3985	4465
115	2320	3030	4085	4565
120	2385	3105	4185	4665
125	2450	3180	4285	4765
130	2515	3255	4385	4865
135	2580	3330	4485	4965
140	2645	3405	4585	5065
145	2710	3480	4685	5165
150	2775	3555	4785	5265
155	2840	3630	4885	5365
160	2905	3705	4985	5465
165	2970	3780	5085	5565
170	3035	3855	5185	5665
175	3100	3930	5285	5765
180	3165	4005	5385	5865
185	3230	4080	5485	5965
190	3295	4155	5585	6065
195	3360	4230	5685	6165
200	3425	4305	5785	6265
205	3490	4380	5885	6365
210	3555	4455	5985	6465
215	3620	4530	6085	6565
220	3685	4605	6185	6665
225	3750	4680	6285	6765
230	3815	4755	6385	6865
235	3880	4830	6485	6965
240	3945	4905	6585	7065
245	4010	4980	6685	7165
250	4075	5055	6785	7265
255	4140	5130	6885	7365

MAINTAIN WEIGHT
Calories allowed per day

LBS	Hours of exercise 0	1	2	3
70	910	1530	2360	2840
75	975	1605	2460	2940
80	1040	1680	2560	3040
85	1105	1755	2660	3140
90	1170	1860	2760	3240
95	1235	1905	2860	3340
100	1300	1980	2960	3440
105	1365	2055	3060	3540
110	1430	2130	3160	3640
115	1495	2205	3260	3740
120	1560	2280	3360	3840
125	1625	2355	3460	3940
130	1690	2430	3560	4040
135	1755	2505	3660	4140
140	1820	2580	3760	4240
145	1885	2655	3860	4340
150	1950	2730	3960	4440
155	2015	2805	4060	4540
160	2080	2880	4160	4640
165	2145	2955	4260	4740
170	2210	3030	4360	4840
175	2275	3105	4460	4940
180	2340	3180	4560	5040
185	2405	3255	4660	5140
190	2470	3330	4760	5240
195	2535	3405	4860	5340
200	2600	3480	4960	5440
205	2665	3555	5060	5540
210	2730	3630	5160	5640
215	2795	3705	5260	5740
220	2860	3780	5360	5840
225	2925	3855	5460	5940
230	2990	3930	5560	6040
235	3055	4005	5660	6140
240	3120	4080	5760	6240
245	3185	4155	5860	6340
250	3250	4230	5960	6440
255	3315	4305	6060	6540
260	3380	4380	6160	6640
265	3445	4455	6260	6740
270	3510	4530	6360	6840
275	3575	4605	6460	6940

CALORIE CHART FOR MEN

WEIGHT LOSS
Calories allowed per day

LBS	0	1	2	3
115	1000	1325	2500	3100
120	1000	1400	2600	3200
125	1000	1475	2700	3300
130	1000	1550	2800	3400
135	1000	1625	2900	3500
140	1000	1700	3000	3600
145	1000	1775	3100	3700
150	1000	1850	3200	3800
155	1015	1925	3300	3900
160	1080	2000	3400	4000
165	1145	2075	3500	4100
170	1210	2150	3600	4200
175	1275	2225	3700	4300
180	1340	2300	3800	4400
185	1405	2375	3900	4500
190	1470	2450	4000	4600
195	1535	2525	4100	4700
200	1600	2600	4200	4800
205	1665	2675	4300	4900
210	1730	2750	4400	5000
215	1795	2825	4500	5100
220	1860	2900	4600	5200
225	1925	2925	4700	5300
230	1990	3050	4800	5400
235	2055	3125	4900	5500
240	2120	3200	5000	5600
245	2185	3275	5100	5700
250	2250	3350	5200	5800
255	2315	3425	5300	5900
260	2380	3500	5400	6060
265	2445	3575	5500	6100
270	2510	3650	5600	6200
275	2575	3725	5700	6300
280	2640	3800	5800	6400
285	2705	3875	5900	6500
290	2770	3950	6060	6600
295	2835	4025	6100	6700
300	2900	4100	6200	6800

WEIGHT GAIN
Calories allowed per day

LBS	0	1	2	3
80	1865	2625	3625	4225
85	1930	2700	3725	4325
90	1995	2775	3825	4425
95	2060	2850	3925	4525
100	2125	2925	4250	4625
105	2190	3000	4125	4725
110	2255	3075	4225	4825
115	2320	3150	4325	4925
120	2385	3335	4425	5250
125	2450	3300	4525	5125
130	2515	3375	4625	5225
135	2580	3450	4725	5325
140	2645	3535	4825	5425
145	2710	3600	4925	5525
150	2775	3675	5250	5625
155	2840	3750	5125	5725
160	2905	3835	5225	5825
165	2970	3900	5325	5925
170	3035	3935	5425	6060
175	3100	4050	5525	6125
180	3165	4125	5625	6225
185	3230	4200	5725	6325
190	3295	4275	5825	6425
195	3660	4450	5925	6525
200	3425	4425	6060	6625
205	3490	4500	6125	6725
210	3555	4575	6225	6825
215	3620	4650	6325	6925
220	3685	4725	6425	7250
225	3750	4800	6525	7125
230	3815	4875	6625	7225
235	3880	4950	6725	7325
240	3945	5025	6825	7425
245	4010	5100	6925	7525
250	4075	5175	7250	7625
255	4140	5250	7125	7725
260	4205	5325	7225	7825
265	4270	5400	7325	7925
270	4335	5475	7425	8025
275	4400	5550	7525	8125
280	4465	5625	7625	8225
285	4530	5700	7725	8325

MAINTAIN WEIGHT
Calories allowed per day

LBS	0	1	2	3
90	1170	1950	3000	3600
95	1235	2025	3100	3700
100	1300	2100	3200	3800
105	1365	2175	3300	3900
110	1430	2250	3400	4000
115	1495	2325	3500	4100
120	1560	2400	3600	4200
125	1625	2475	3700	4300
130	1690	2550	3800	4400
135	1755	2625	3900	4500
140	1820	2700	4000	4600
145	1885	2775	4100	4700
150	1950	2850	4200	4800
155	2015	2925	4300	4900
160	2080	3000	4400	5000
165	2145	3075	4500	5100
170	2210	3150	4600	5200
175	2275	3225	4700	5300
180	2340	3300	4800	5400
185	2405	3375	4900	5500
190	2470	3450	5000	5600
195	2535	3525	5100	5700
200	2600	3600	5200	5800
205	2665	3675	5300	5900
210	2730	3750	5400	6000
215	2795	3825	5500	6100
220	2860	3900	5600	6200
225	2925	3975	5700	6300
230	2990	4050	5800	6400
235	3055	4125	5900	6500
240	3120	4200	6000	6600
245	3185	4275	6100	6700
250	3250	4350	6200	6800
255	3315	4425	6300	6900
260	3380	4500	6400	7000
265	3450	4575	6500	7100
270	3510	4650	6600	7200
275	3575	4725	6700	7300
280	3640	4800	6800	7400
285	3705	4875	6900	7500
290	3770	4950	7000	7600
295	3835	5025	7100	7700
300	3900	5100	7200	7800

FOOD PYRAMID

How many times have you seen this pyramid on a label and ignored it? This is called the food pyramid. A more detailed picture of it is on the following page. The pyramid shows a sample of how the breakdown of your daily nutrients should be. If you look at it closely, it will show you visually exactly how this book has been encouraging you to eat. Notice on the diagram below, just what a large role carbohydrates play in our daily nutrition. This is our main energy source. The food pyramid shows serving sizes, but does not consider the calorie or fat content, so it can only be used as a guide if you are trying to lose or gain weight.

The food pyramid shows serving size in more detail to help you get a better idea of serving proportions.

Food Guide Pyramid
A Guide to Daily Food Choices

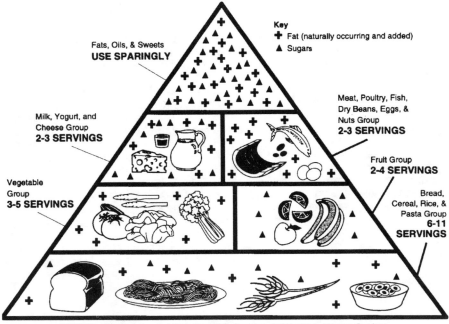

Key
+ Fat (naturally occurring and added)
▲ Sugars

Fats, Oils, & Sweets
USE SPARINGLY

Meat, Poultry, Fish, Dry Beans, Eggs, & Nuts Group
2-3 SERVINGS

Milk, Yogurt, and Cheese Group
2-3 SERVINGS

Fruit Group
2-4 SERVINGS

Vegetable Group
3-5 SERVINGS

Bread, Cereal, Rice, & Pasta Group
6-11 SERVINGS

SOURCE: U.S. Department of Agriculture. U.S. Department of Health and Human Services.

How Many Servings Do You Need Each Day?

Use these ranges as your guide for how much food to eat each day. Choose the lower or higher number of servings based on your calorie needs. If you eat more or less than one serving, count as partial servings. For children under 5, one serving is generally 1/4 - 1/3 of an adult serving.

Fats, Oils & Sweets
USE SPARINGLY

Sometimes Foods
These foods provide little or no nutrition and are often high in fat, sugar, salt and calories. They should be eaten in moderation and not in place of servings from the five food groups.

Milk, Yougurt, & Cheese Group: 2-3 Servings/day
ONE SERVING IS: 1 cup (8oz) milk, 2 slices cheese, 1/2 cup ricotta cheese, 2 cups cottage cheese, 1 1/2 cups frozen yogurt

Meat, Poultry, Fish Dry Beans, Eggs and Nuts Group 2-3 Servings/day
ONE SERVING IS: 2-3 ounces cooked meat, fish or 2 eggs, 7 oz. tofu, 1 cup cooked beans, 1/2 cup nuts poultry or seeds, 4 tbl. peanut butter

Vegetable Group 3-5 Servings
ONE SERVING IS: 1/2 cup cooked vegetables, 1/2 cup raw vegetables, 1 cup raw leafy vegetables, 1/2 - 3/4 cup juice

Fruit Group 2-4 Servings
ONE SERVING IS: 1 whole fruit, 1/2/ cup canned fruit, 1/4 cup dried fruit, 1/2 - 3/4 cup juice

Bread, Cereal, Rice & Pasta Group 6-11 Servings
ONE SERVING IS: 1 slice bread, 1 medium muffin, 4 small crackers, 1 cup ready-to-eat cereal 1/3 - 1/2 cup cooked or granola type cereal, 1/2 cup pasta or rice, 1 tortilla, 1/2 hot dog or hamburger bun, 1/2 bagel or English muffin.

MILK = 1/2 Serving
MEAT = 0 Servings
VEGETABLES = 0 Servings
FRUITS = 2 Servings
BREADS & CEREALS = 2 Servings

MILK = 2 Serving
MEAT = 1 Servings
VEGETABLES = 1/2 Servings
FRUITS = 1 Servings
BREADS & CEREALS = 2 Servings

MILK = 1 Serving
MEAT = 1 Serving
VEGETABLES = 2 1/2 Servings
FRUITS = 0 Servings
BREADS & CEREALS = 2 Servings

MEAL TIMING

*Snack time
is just as
important
as meal time.*

You are thinking, what is meal timing? This is one of the keys to help you lose or gain weight more effectively. Your biochemistry is a very balanced piece of machinery. You need to think of food as FUEL. It's always important to keep fuel in our bodies so that we can have energy for the day. The problem with DIETS are they cut back on your fuel, or don't give you the nutrients your body needs, and the time between getting that fuel is too far between. This is going to take some time and organization at first, but like anything else it gets easier as you go.

As said before, most Americans have this preconceived idea of three square meals a day. This is dated from earlier days. Times and life styles have changed since then, and people today are much more on the go. The ideal is to be able to eat four to six SMALL meals all day long. The reason being, blood sugar levels do dramatic highs and lows when food is held back, then a meal is eaten. Energy levels become sporadic and the body's metabolism goes into flip flops. Let's use the horse again for an example. You'd like to go riding ALL day. You saddle up, get on and take off, but you've forgotten to feed the horse. He's too tired. You are having to kick the horse to get him going. He started out with no fuel so he has no energy.

You figure this out about mid-morning and stop to feed him. You get back on for your ride, and find he's full of life and energy now, and ride for a few hours. You've passed lunch by this time, because you're having so much fun, but you're having to kick and kick him again to get him going. You stop for a snack and give him an apple. You head back in and decide to just run. You run and run but then, all of a sudden, the horse poops out, and stops. You're frustrated because it's no fun any longer, so you give up and go back home. Think of your body as the horse's body. Is this what you do to yourself all day? Forget to eat? No time to eat? You've exhausted your metabolism and body by now.

"Eating all this food just makes me crazy."

Now, let's look at the healthy way to eat! You saddle up the horse and remember to feed him before the long ride. You get on, noticing he's ready to go. You ride for a few hours, and get off to rest and give him a bite of grass to eat. After resting, you ride again for another few hours, full of energy, and enjoying the ride. You stop for lunch, and let him eat more grass while you have your lunch. Again, you get on and decide to run and play. After a few hours you rest at the top of the hill before going back. The horse leans over to eat grass again. You want to run all the way home, and this time the horse doesn't stop until he's home.

Can you see the difference? The first horse is not eating consistently through the day, and continuously runs out of energy. The second horse never runs out of energy. Our bodies work in the same manner. If we don't continually fuel our bodies through the day our metabolism will go off balance causing our energy levels to be sporadic, possibly causing recurring fatigue. Consistent small meals about every 2 to 3 hours gives the body an even amount of fuel to run all day, not giving the blood sugar levels a chance to rise and drop dramatically. They also give us the vitamin and mineral nutrients that we need through the day. By not eating in a consistent pattern, it throws our bodies off making them work too hard, causing fatigue, mood swings, and even poor health.

Your caloric count for the day will determine how often your meals will be. You're now saying you don't have time and your schedule is too busy. Work meals in the best you can, and try to eat as many times as available that your schedule allows. That may mean carrying some snacks in your purse, car, or wherever you need to. You don't have time to prepare these little meals every day? Neither do I, so my aunt taught me an old trick that she still uses today. When making a meal (for example: The Onion Chicken dish on page xxx) if the recipe calls for 4 thighs (servings for 1 or 2) prepare it for 4 or 6 to have extra to freeze. Figure what equals your one meal (adding the right quantity of rice and vegetable), place in plastic containers, and freeze for later use. You have future meals prepared and less chance for you to cheat. It sounds like a lot of work. It's really not! In the long run you save time. You're learning how to prepare, measure and understand how low fat eating really works for you. If you are a person that doesn't have that kind of time, pick things that will take a short time to prepare. Recipes in the cookbook section have preparation times for your convenience. Prepare them the night before, or early in the morning. BUT the key is to make your whole day (or week's) preparations all at once if you are going to be too busy that day. This will help eliminate the possibility of cheating by eating in a restaurant or picking up junk food.

If only 3 meals can be accomplished in the day, make breakfast the largest. Breakfast starts your metabolism off to a good start. This will start you with enough energy to make it through the day. Dinner should be fairly small. If you are going to eat after dinner, make sure you don't eat too late, leaving 2 to 3 hours before bedtime without eating. If you really have to eat a snack in the evening, make it from the carbohydrate family, as these are easier to digest. NO BED TIME SNACKING. Have you ever eaten before going to bed, and woken up tired? Or, have you ever eaten sugar before going to bed and had some really strange dreams? Well, when you go to bed with food in your stomach your mind may rest while sleeping, but your body is hard at work trying to digest that food, and doesn't get the chance to fully rest. This throws your biological clock off, and when you awake, you're tired, because your body has worked all night. Complete rest is important to the body and mind to optimize their function and balance in handling any of the daily challenges or stresses you will give it. If rest is not obtained, the body and mind can slowly break down and the simplest daily decisions can become the most difficult, stressful and frustrating; not to mention your body may have more physical problems.

Meals should be eaten every 2 to 3 hours.

So, timing your fuel and rest are important. Find out what works best for you and be CONSISTENT. Consistency is the key! Your body's clock will click into this new pattern and you will see a new, healthier you. From this section take with you: Eat smaller more frequent meals, breakfast is the most important meal, AND NO bedtime snacks.

DAILY MENU PLAN

BREAKFAST:	FOOD CHOICES	EXCHANGES
Starch Exchange:	1/3 C. Bran cereal	1 Exchange
Fruit Exchange:	1/2 Grapefruit	1 Exchange
Dairy Exchange:	1 C. 1 % Milk	1 Exchange

Total Meal Calories: 245

AM SNACK:	FOOD CHOICES	EXCHANGES
Starch Exchange:	8 Animal Crackers	1 Exchange
Fruit Exchange:	1 Apple (2" across)	1 Exchange

Total Meal Calories 160

LUNCH:	FOOD CHOICES	EXCHANGES
Protein (low fat) Exchange:	5 oz. Sirloin	5 Exchanges
Vegetable Exchange:	1 1/2 C. Carrots	3 Exchanges
Starch Exchange:	1 sm. Potato, baked	1 Exchange
Fruit Exchange:	1 Orange	1 Exchange
Dairy Exchange:	8 oz. Yogurt, plain, nonfat	1 Exchange

Total Meal Calories: 616

PM SNACK:	FOOD CHOICES	EXCHANGES
Vegetable Exchange:	1/2 C. Celery	1 Exchange
Starch Exchange:	3 Graham crackers	1 Exchange
Fruit Exchange:	1/2 Banana (9" long)	1 Exchange

Total Meal Calories: 192

DINNER:	FOOD CHOICES	EXCHANGES
Protein (low fat) Exchange:	8 oz. Chicken, skinned	8 Exchanges
Vegetable Exchange:	1 1/2 C. Asparagus	3 Exchanges
Starch Exchange:	1/2 C. Corn + 2/3 C Rice	3 Exchanges
Fruit Exchange:	30 Grapes	1 Exchange

Total Meal Calories: 936

DAILY TOTAL CALORIES: 2149

EXERCISE

Along with the new knowledge you have about eating habits, exercise is imperative to lose or gain weight and maintain a healthy lifestyle. There are many benefits to exercise, no matter what kind of exercise you choose:

- Exercise releases stress.

- Increases longevity.

- Reduces body fat.

- Helps cholesterol (increases HDL, the good cholesterol).

- Increases energy.

- Helps mental state.

Most of the people that have yo-yo dieted, likely have not incorporated much physical activity. If exercise IS NOT incorporated it will be much more difficult to lose or gain the weight. Exercising does not take much time. It is a misconceived idea that a person must exercise for 1 or 2 hours to get total benefits. This is not true. It's only necessary to keep your pulse rate up in what is called the target zone, (explained in the next section) for a minimum of 20 minutes. If you desire to do more, that is up to you. The Target Zone is the optimum time period for cardiovascular aerobic activity. There should be a warm up period and light stretching for 5 minutes before, and a 5 minute cool down period after, to give your heart a chance to speed up and slow down gradually, not to shock it by completely stopping suddenly as this can cause damage. So, your total activity time may be as little as 30 minutes or more, that depends on you.

Exercise should fit your life style, and if you've been inactive for a period of time it's <u>extremely important</u> to start out SLOWLY and gradually increase. Often, the people who start new diets and exercise programs go "gung ho" in the beginning and after about the 3rd week start feeling deprived, frustrated or burned out. If they continue at a high pace, they may just give up all together. This is the opposite of what we are trying to accomplish. Exercise will help your caloric intake. You'll be able to eat MORE, rather than resorting to the old idea of starving yourself. Exercise will even help with stress, moodiness and fatigue. Yes, you'll have more energy, not less.

A good indication of whether or not you're over-exercising during aerobic activity, is if you're able to hold a conversation without being out of breath. If you are panting or having difficulty breathing while talking, you are exercising too hard. You should be able to carry on a normal conversation. If you can't, slow your activity down until you can. Exercising at this pace should put you in your target zone. Check your pulse rate to be sure. Remember, don't try to jump into a heavy aerobic workout if you haven't been exercising for awhile.

Be sure to pick an exercise activity that you WILL ENJOY. Too often, people think they have to join a gym to exercise even if they truly don't want to. Exercise comes in many forms, so find one that you enjoy. You will do it much longer and be more likely to keep it in your new lifestyle. If you pick something that you don't enjoy, you will constantly watch the clock and dread doing it the next time you have to. You'll be more likely to ultimately quit the program and go back to your old life style.

"Don't be intimidated by exercise, I'm not."

56

CALORIE EXPENDITURES

PER HOUR AND MINUTE

ACTIVITY	HR	MIN	ACTIVITY	HR	MIN
Aerobics - moderate	262.2	4.37	Painting - building	177.0	2.95
- vigorous	361.8	6.03	Plastering	177.0	2.95
Badminton	241.2	4.02	Racquetball - leisure	439.8	7.33
Baseball	148.8	2.48	- intense	574.2	9.57
Basketball - moderate	297.6	4.96	Running - 12 min. mile	333.0	5.55
- vigorous	411.0	6.85	- 9 min. mile	553.2	9.22
Bicycling - 10 mph	319.2	5.32	- 6 min. mile	744.0	12.4
- 6 mph	156.0	2.60	Sawing - hand	319.2	5.32
Billiards	63.6	1.06	- power	170.4	2.84
Bowling	141.6	2.36	Scrubbing floors	283.8	4.73
Boxing - sparring	375.6	6.26	Shoveling	205.8	3.43
Callisthenics	163.2	2.72	Skating - moderate	198.6	3.31
Canoeing - leisurely	78.0	1.30	Skiing - cross country	538.8	8.98
Carrying logs	531.6	8.86	- down hill leisure	282.8	4.73
Chopping wood - fast	618.0	10.3	- downhill intense	460.8	7.68
- slow	205.8	3.43	Skindiving - moderate	557.4	9.29
Cleaning	127.8	2.13	- vigorous	708.0	7.68
Cooking	78.0	1.30	Snowshoeing	460.8	11.8
Dancing - moderate	141.6	2.36	Soccer - moderate	347.4	5.79
- vigorous	319.2	5.32	- vigorous	411.0	6.85
Fishing	127.8	2.13	Squash	612.0	10.2
Food shopping	127.8	2.13	Stacking firewood	213.0	3.55
Football	354.6	5.91	Strength training	283.8	4.73
Free weights	205.8	3.43	Swimming - fast	432.6	7.21
Gardening - digging	333.0	5.55	- slow	340.2	5.67
- mowing	291.0	4.85	Table tennis - leisure	283.8	4.73
- raking	106.2	1.77	Treading water	319.2	5.32
Golfing	205.8	3.43	Trimming trees	347.4	5.79
Gymnastics - moderate	141.6	2.36	Universal weights	304.8	5.08
- vigorous	354.6	5.91	Volleyball - leisure	92.4	1.54
Handball	382.8	6.38	- intense	163.2	2.72
Hiking	213.0	3.55	Walking - normal pace	184.2	3.07
Horseback riding - walk	63.6	1.06	- vigorous	248.4	4.14
gallop	369.0	6.15	Weeding	163.2	2.72
Ironing	85.2	1.42	Window Cleaning	113.4	1.89
Judo	560.4	9.34	Wrestling	531.6	8.86

CALORIES BURNED PER HOUR

DANCING
319 Calories

SKIING
284 Calories

WASHING A CAR
128 Calories

RUNNING
333 Calories

WEIGHT TRAINING
304 Calories

TARGET ZONE

The target zone is the area where FAT is burned. The idea is not to exercise too much beyond where you are burning the fat and end up burning muscle tissue. The target zone is MODERATE exercise. We find thee Target Zone by using our maximum Heart Rate (MHR). This is determined by our age, not how fit you are. A simple and semi-accurate way to figure your maximum heart rate is

$$\frac{220}{-AGE}$$
$$=MHR \text{ (maximum heart rate)}$$

For a more accurate calculation follow the chart on page 60. When exercising, the ideal is NOT to hit your MHR, but to stay in 70-85% of it. That is YOUR target zone! Staying there for 20 minutes will ensure you to burn fat.

How can you tell if you are in your target zone? During exercise, stop, place your first 3 fingers where you can feel your pulse either on your wrist or on the sides of the center bone of the neck (slightly on the side below the jaw bone). Press lightly Not much pressure is needed. Take the count for 10 seconds and multiply times six. This gives you your heart rate for one minute.

"If someone offers you Baloney. . .
take it, roll it up and make a hot dog."

FINDING YOUR TARGET HEART RATE

Heart Rate (Pulse): The number of times your heart beats in one minute. This indicates the level of exertion the heart is experiencing.

Resting Heart Rate: The number of times your heart beats in one minute when you truly are at rest. The best time to take this measurement is before you get out of bed in the morning; when you've had a good night's sleep and you're not feeling rushed. A well conditioned person's resting heart rate will be 45 - 60 beats per minute.

Fat burning Heart Rate: This heart rate allows you to utilize FAT as a primary energy source during aerobic exercise. This rate is 60% of your age and resting heart rate adjusted maximum heart rate.

Exercise Heart Rate: This heart rate allows you to achieve greater cardio-pulmonary benefits. This rate is 80% of your age and resting heart rate adjusted maximum heart rate.

Maximum Heart Rate: The highest number of beats per minute your heart can beat. This level of exertion should not be sustained as it is potentially dangerous.

Target Heart Rate: This is a range between 60% and 80% of your age and resting heart rate adjusted maximum heart rate. This range guarantees that you will receive the benefits of aerobic exercise.

TARGET HEART RATE FORMULA

TO FIND YOUR **FAT BURNING** HEART RATE 60% INTENSITY	TO FIND YOUR **EXERCISE** HEART RATE 80% INTENSITY
220 Start with this number	220 Start with this number
-_____Subtract your age from 220	-_____Subtract your age from 220
=_____Your maximum heart rate	=_____Your maximum heart rate
-_____Subtract resting heart rate	-_____Subtract resting heart rate
=_____	=_____
X_____Multiply by 60% (.60)	X_____Multiply by 80% (.80)
=_____	=_____
+_____Add your resting heart rate	+_____Add your resting heart rate
=_____Your fat burning heart rate	=_____Your exercise heart rate

GOAL SETTING

Goals are important for your progress and keep you on track. First, your goals must be realistic and achievable. Remember, you're trying to lose a maximum of only two to three pounds a week. Set daily, weekly and monthly goals so you won't become discouraged. Changing your way of life will take time. Remember how much time it took you to develop all the habits you have now, so don't expect yourself to change overnight. If you do, you are setting yourself up for failure. Most people with weight problems have had them for years and years, so BE GENTLE with yourself. Don't expect too much from yourself, too fast. If you fall back a day or two, don't beat yourself up over it and feel guilty. Say, "O.K., I fell off yesterday, but today I'm getting back on the horse." Weight problems are like any other problems. Take them DAY BY DAY. You get through one day at a time, and don't worry about the next until it is here. Make your goals to suit you, since each person is different. If it helps to write your goals down, and cross them off as you accomplish them, then do so.

HELPFUL HINTS TO MEET YOUR GOALS

- Keep a note of your eating patterns for the first week. When are the times that you tend to eat the most?

- Do you come home straight from work, go to the kitchen and open the refrigerator? Determine why you do this. Are your actions caused by EMOTIONS or HUNGER? Watch what kind of moods set you off to eat more. Our emotions play an enormous role in our eating habits. Are you eating because you're bored, angry, frustrated, lonely, hurt or stressed out? If it helps, put a sign on your refrigerator to make you think before opening the door. ONLY EAT WHEN YOU ARE PHYSICALLY HUNGRY. Stick to your plan. STOP, THINK, DECIDE.

61

- Let friends and family know that you are changing your eating lifestyle and not dieting. Make them aware that this is a new life pattern, not a diet. Request they don't offer any sweets or fattening foods. This will take time for them and in the beginning they will offer, but when they see you are serious and your body is changing, they will become interested and want to know more about what you are doing. They will realize you are serious and stop giving you those temptations. CHANGE IS GOOD, but humans don't like change and they are reluctant until they get used to the idea. It took my family and friends a long time to accept my new way because they had seen me fail on diets so many times before. But because I was consistent, stuck to my goals and continued my new lifestyle, they accepted it. Now it's been years, and they come to me to find out how they can change or modify a recipe to a healthier style.

- When eating out at a restaurant, keep to the low fat foods. Ask the waiter or waitress if there is a diabetic or low fat diet plate (many restaurants have "light" meals, which are low fat). If needed, explain to the waitress what you are doing. If you are a regular customer in that restaurant the waiter or waitress will pick up on your new habit. Most restaurants will try to accommodate your needs.

- When traveling by air, ask the airline in advance if they have diabetic or vegetarian meals. Most do, but need you to request them ahead of time. When on vacation it's O.K. to splurge in moderation, but get right back into the new habits when you return.

- Temptations will always be there, and it's discipline that needs to take over. Conquer weakness by continually telling yourself NO, and taking an alternative if there is one available. If there's no alternative, go outside, take a walk, call up a friend for support, get active with SOMETHING to get your mind off food.

- When grocery shopping, make a list before going and stick to the list. GET ONLY WHAT'S ON YOUR LIST. If you are hungry, eat before you go shopping. Most impulsive shopping is done because you're hungry and everything looks good. READ the LABELS!!!

- Stick to your exercise plan. If you missed a day, just get back on the horse the next day. Don't beat yourself up, and make yourself feel guilty.

- Carry healthy foods or snacks with you to eliminate the possibilities of cheating, and stick to your goals.

- Remember CONSISTENCY is the key to changing and keeping your goals.

"Knowledge is important. . . but what you do with it is what counts."

*PHYSICALLY CHALLENGED?*_____

Pregnancy, physical disabilities, or poor physical health has limitations, but with your doctors consent and supervision, slower, easier activities, such as water aerobics, can be a gentle way to exercise. Water helps support your body, is gentle on the joints, and is low impact. Water has more resistance, therefore you get more of a workout than on land. Many pools these days are set up for handicapped, with lifts to help ease you into the water. Contact your local recreation center for this information. Most have classes for physically challenged individuals. If you are unsure of what to do or where to go, check your local yellow pages or ask for help at a local park and recreation facility. They can direct you.

"Jump over the hurdle and give it a try.

Never give up!"

PREGNANCY

PREGNANCY AND NUTRITION

Whether preparing for pregnancy or while during pregnancy, this is not the time to try to alter your weight. It's a time to manage your weight and eat as healthy as you can. So that your body and baby both have the best chances for a healthy start in new life.

When you take responsibility for another person from the beginning there are precautions that you will want to take. Talking to your physician about every detail will reassure you. Speaking with a registered dietitian will insure that you are giving both the baby and yourself all the nutrients necessary for staying healthy.

During your pregnancy it is important to make sure that you are getting ENOUGH to eat, as well as a nutritionally balanced diet. Your body amazingly, will tell you what your nutritional needs are through cravings. For example: Maybe, you suddenly crave milk. Your body may be a little low on calcium or protein or both. Cravings may not be as significant as this example, but at this time it's important to pay close attention to what you are putting into your body.

Other cravings may turn you against particular foods and cause you to lose of all desire for them. This will gradually change, and the desire will return either during the pregnancy, or after the baby is born.

There are some foods you are used to eating that your doctor may ask you to avoid during pregnancy. It is important to heed this advice, as certain foods eaten frequently may damage the baby's health. Below are just a few:

- **CAFFEINE:** Coffee, colas and certain teas.

- **ARTIFICIAL SWEETENERS:** At this time it's better to use real sugars.

- **ALCOHOL:** Any and all.

- **ADDITIVES AND PRESERVATIVES:** Including artificial colorings, artificial flavoring and MSG (monosodium glutamate).

It is most important to try and avoid these during the first trimester when the baby is forming in all aspects. Remember, natural eating is best.

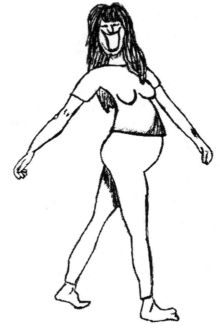

"Consider a river. . . it follows a path of least resistance and it's always crooked."

PREGNANCY AND A BALANCED DIET

During pregnancy, as in your daily life, your diet should include the basics of the Food Pyramid, covered in the Food Pyramid section on pages 76 and 77. Pregnancy is a time to follow the basics, along with adding extra servings of certain groups to help the baby grow strong.

You're probably asking the same questions I did, "How many more calories should I be eating?" The average is to eat approximately 300 to 400 more calories than you did before becoming pregnant. Say your daily consumption was 1700 calories without exercising. You may add about 300 more calories to that taking your total up to 2000 calories a day. Remember the old saying, "You're eating for two?" Well, just remember how little that second person is. He or she is NOT a full grown person. This is where many women falter, and think they can eat anything they want because they are pregnant. WRONG! It's still wise to stay within moderation when it comes to extra helpings of this or that and analyze your cravings. It will make it harder for you to work off the extra weight after the baby is born, if you splurged all through your pregnancy. Be sure to consult with your physician as to the specific calorie consumption best for you and your needs.

With the increase of calories there will be an unavoidable increase in fat. As I have said before, this is not a time to worry about weight reduction. You will increase fats by eating more protein (which the baby needs for muscle development), dairy products (for strong bone formation), and carbohydrates (as you will need these for energy).

As your pregnancy proceeds, your appetite will increase as the baby grows and needs more nutrition. As my mother told me through my craving stages, "Honey, you just wait. You'll want to attach the refrigerator to your wrist." You'll sometimes feel that way.

One of the MOST important things to remember through the whole course of your pregnancy is to GET ENOUGH WATER. Drink, drink and drink some more. Taking in fluids is so vital at this point, as the fluid surrounding the baby changes every few hours. Not drinking enough water, will also make you dehydrated and unhealthy. Water exchanges in your body are extremely important at this time. If you begin to retain too much water, ask yourself how much water are you drinking a day. Remember to drink at least 6 to 8, 8 ounce glasses a day. It sounds strange, but it takes water to flush water out of your system. If you continue to retain water consult your physician, as something else may be going on with you and your baby.

DECREASE YOUR SALT INTAKE, as salt also tends to retain water. Try eating a low salt diet if you aren't already. If you haven't ever eaten a low salt diet the food will taste a little more bland, but you'll become used to it.

Here are just a few guidelines about servings during your pregnancy. Refer again to the food pyramid section if you need help with serving sizes:

FOOD GROUPS	PER DAY
PROTEIN GROUP:	2 to 3 servings.
MILK GROUP:	AT LEAST 4 servings.
VEGETABLE GROUP:	3 to 5 servings.
FRUIT GROUP:	2 to 4 servings.
BREAD, CEREAL, RICE, PASTA:	6 to 11 servings.

So, you can see there is a lot more food eaten while you are pregnant. Making meals smaller and more frequent in the beginning will make it easier on you later in your pregnancy, because as the baby grows, (and grows upward) it will become much harder to eat larger meals. Smaller more frequent meals will also help prevent the possibility of heartburn.

DURING PREGNANCY IT'S COMMON
TO GAIN 24 TO 30 POUNDS.

Pregnancy and weight gain should be gradual. Rapid weight gain, if you are watching what you eat, could indicate something is wrong, and you should let your physician know. During pregnancy it's common to gain approximately 24 to 30 pounds. It's very normal, and also recommended. The following is an example of the distribution of weight a baby adds:

	Pounds
Baby	7.5
Placenta	1.0
Amniotic fluid	2.0
Breast tissue	1.0
Uterus	2.5
Blood	3.5
Other fluids	2.75
Other	3.25
Total:	23.5 pounds

Here is an example of typical weight increase:

- The first trimester (from 1 to 3 months) an average of 3 to 4 total pounds will be gained.
- The second trimester (from 4 to 6 months) an average of 10 to 12 total pounds will be gained.
- In the last trimester (from 7 to 9 months) an average of 11 to 14 total pounds will be gained.

It is essential to gain weight during pregnancy. If you try to diet, it can affect your health as well as the baby's.

PREGNANCY AND SUPPLEMENTS

During your pregnancy your physician may either prescribe Prenatal vitamins or give you samples to try. You may ask, "If I'm eating right, then why do I need prenatal vitamins?" Even if you are paying close attention, you can miss essential vitamins the baby needs (such as Iron or folic acid). Regular daily vitamins normally don't contain the extra vitamins and minerals necessary for the baby's growth and development. Your doctor may recommend fluoride tablets to help the baby's tooth development if your water system is lacking in flouride.

If you are taking vitamins and have questions about them, bring the vitamins in with you to the doctor and ask about them. The doctor will tell you if your vitamins are sufficient for you and the development of the baby. The doctor is there for you and to help in the growth of a healthy baby.

PREGNANCY AND EXERCISE

Just because you are pregnant does not mean you should stop exercising. During the first trimester (the first 3 months), you may not be well enough (due to morning sickness) to feel like exercising. Getting out when you can for some fresh air may help you a little. When you are feeling well again, it's time to get back into the routine of exercise.

Exercise will change during the stages of pregnancy, as it will become more difficult to do certain moves. If you haven't exercised before, start out very slowly and work your way up. DON'T OVER DO IT!!!!! Even if you are used to exercise it's important that you watch your heart rate, as you may be used to a much higher rate than what you need to keep it at during pregnancy. YOUR HEART RATE SHOULD STAY AT OR BELOW 140 BEATS PER MINUTE.

Pulse rate should be taken periodically during your workout so that you can be sure that you are keeping within the guidelines. Placing your finger tips either on your wrist or on the side of the Adam's apple on your neck, you should be able to take your pulse. Count for 10 seconds. This is a quick way to figure your heart rate. The following is an approximate guide:

AGE	BEATS PER 10 SECONDS
20 - 25	20 - 23
26 - 30	19 - 22
31 - 35	18 - 22
36 - 40	18 - 21
31 - 45	17 - 20

*NOTE: Before, during or after exercising if there is any cramping, bleeding or pain, exercise should be stopped. You should contact your physician to be sure the exercise is not hurting you or the baby.

DURING EXERCISE YOUR HEART RATE SHOULD BE 140 BEATS PER MINUTE OR LESS.

These are some benefits of exercising during pregnancy:

- Helps stabilize your metabolism.

- Lessens irritability and restlessness.

- Helps keep your mental state positive while your body is going through all the physical changes.

- It can help make a smoother labor, and in some cases, shorter.

PREGNANCY AND YOUR MENTAL STATE

Pregnancy is a time for mental and physical changes. It is wise to read as much as you can about pregnancy to help you understand the changes your mind and body will go through. This will help you to relax and understand what is happening to your body is normal.

Keeping a positive attitude throughout your pregnancy is very important for the health of your baby, as well. Stress and restlessness can have negative affects and should be avoided as much as possible. Of course, daily stresses are always there, but avoid additional stress if possible.

Giving yourself pats on the back as you go will help your self esteem. If you have a partner let that person know you'll need a little more encouragement during the times you are not feeling your best.

Emotionally, you'll have up and down days, and it's important not to worry too much about the down days. Both your body and your mind are going through extensive chemical changes. On the down days, try to cheer yourself up by doing something you enjoy, or by talking to someone who will help cheer you up. Eat healthy and enjoy your pregnancy.

Just remember, IT WON'T LAST!

MAINTAINING THE NEW YOU

Getting Off the Horse and Moving On

Now that you have some knowledge to get you started on how to eat healthy and get to the desired weight you've always dreamed of, you need to maintain it. Getting to this point was the hard part because you had to learn all new habits, gain pride in yourself along the way, find a new exercise program to suit you, and get through the negatives surrounding you. All of this meant using a lot of discipline.

GOOD JOB GOOD JOB GOOD JOB GOOD JOB

If I could reach through this book and hug you, I would. More importantly, I want you to wrap your arms around yourself and give yourself a hug. You deserve it! You did it for YOU, and I'm sure you are feeling better, if not great! Doesn't it feel good?

The maintenance part is the exact same thing you've been doing all along, except maintaining is easier, as you've already learned the hard part. Well, if it isn't already, it will be! If those negative thoughts are creeping back in, kick them out. You've made it, and now you just need to continue to exercise, and watch what you eat. If you fall back a little, just get right back on the horse as soon as you can.

Vacations, events, and holidays come up, and who doesn't want to join in on the food fun part of it. You'll find though that after eating your healthy new way for about one year, your cravings for the old things will be almost gone if not already done. When you do get that craving and have a Twinkie or Ding Dong, it's not as good as you remembered it, or you'll taste the fat more than you did when you ate it all the time. If you do eat a Twinkie, don't beat yourself up again, just step back and look at yourself as the New You, and say, "I Don't need it anymore."

Remember your weight will fluctuate from 1 to 5 pounds daily, this is very normal. Our water retention and daily consumption will play a part in this. So, DON'T PANIC!! If you notice you are gaining or losing weight again, open this book up and refresh your memory. If needed, go back and do a new menu plan again.

If your emotional state is low, listen to some music that motivates you to get going again or talk to a friend who can boost your self esteem. Listen to motivational tapes or get out and take a walk. Help someone else learn how to eat properly, they'll love you for it in the long run.

DON'T SIT THERE! GET ACTIVE!
BEING ACTIVE CREATES A HEALTHY MENTAL STATE.

Your mental state during the maintaining phase will help you greatly, so continue to try as much as possible to limit stress, keep active and help the next person to a better life.

KEEP UP THE GOOD WORK!
GOOD LUCK ON A NEW HEALTHIER YOU.

"There never has been, or will be another you.
You are rare and special."

COOKING SUBSTITUTIONS_____

This is not difficult once you've become used to the products available on the market. Experimenting is the fun part of cooking. You can stick to the recipes or become creative and use your own ideas. Substituting is comical in my family. Ever since I was a little girl I loved to cook, but many times we didn't have the ingredients needed, so I would find something I could substitute. Sometimes it worked, and sometimes it didn't. After doing this year after year, my mother would ask every time I made something, "What did you substitute?" My family began calling me the "Substitute Queen". Practice makes perfect!

Because we want to stay with natural ingredients as much as possible, this cookbook is slightly different when substituting sugars and oils. Substitutions will be natural if at all possible. Also, product availability depends upon your location and what your supermarket has available. Often times you'll buy a cookbook and it will give you brand names you've never heard of it, or your area doesn't carry them. I don't know how many times I've bought cookbooks and this happens. It's frustrating, because you are excited to try new recipes from the book, and it calls for one ingredient that might be almost impossible to find. Or the cookbook is based on a company's products and THEIR product is in almost every recipe. So, this cookbook, when substituting or modifying, will call for things you may already have in the kitchen, or should be easy to find in your local grocery store. On the following page is a list of substitutions that might help you around the kitchen. This list is also on the substitution sheet and shopping list.

When looking for specific substitutes in your grocery store, ask an employee if the store carries it and if so, where it is located. If the store doesn't have the specific brand, it may have a similar product.

When looking for butter substitutes they will be found in the spice area. It is a good idea to get to know the spice area, even if you are already growing your own spices as many substitutes can be found in this section. Watch labels on butter substitutes or sprays, as some of them can't be substituted in baking.

Be careful when replacing cheeses; most low-fat cheeses don't melt well. Replacing lowfat cheeses 100% will cause your recipes to come out very different. If the cheese is mixed inside a recipe it is not noticeable, but if you are making something with cheese on top, it is better to use a LOW MOISTURE CHEESE.

If you decide to try your own substitutes, try to do them one at a time. If you try to do more than one, and it doesn't turn out, it will be difficult for you to know which one caused the recipe to not turn out.

When wanting to use egg substitutes, try using egg whites. If you use an egg substitute, read the label of the package. They're mostly egg whites. There is a recipe on page 221 for an egg substitute that will save you money, rather than have a company charge you double just add yellow food coloring to egg whites. Remember, the less packaged products, the more natural and more healthy.

SUBSTITUTIONS

Whole egg: 2 egg whites = 1 whole egg
or recipe for egg substitute.

Butter   Butter substitutes - Molly McButter or
Butter Buds.

Cracker crumbs   Toasted oats cereal, Cheerios,
Corn Flakes, Rice Crispies.

Mayonnaise, 1 C.   Fat-free mayonnaise, 1/2 C. low fat
plain yogurt, reduced fat
mayonnaise.

Oil   Low-fat spray or liquid Butter Buds
(not for frying), applesauce, baby
prunes.

Nuts   Grape Nuts cereal or cereal.

Sugar   Sweetener substitutes, juices or
honey.

Chocolate   3 TBS.unsweetened cocoa plus
   (unsweetened)   1 TBS. butter substitute.

Whole Milk, 1 C.   Non-fat milk, dry milk, or 1 Cup of
2%, 1% or skim.

Flour (for thickening)   Arrowroot or Cornstarch.

Dry yeast, 1 Pkg.   1 cake compressed yeast or
2 -1/2 tsp. dry yeast.

Brown sugar   White sugar or double the amount of
powdered sugar.

Buttermilk, 1 C.   1 TBS. lemon juice or vinegar in
enough skim milk to equal one cup.

1 Clove Garlic   1/8 tsp. garlic powder,
or 1/8 tsp. minced <u>dry</u> garlic,
or 1/2 tsp. minced jarred garlic.

Onion (small)	1 tsp. onion powder, or 1 TBS. minced dry onion.
Mustard, 1 TBS. (Prepared)	1 tsp. dry mustard.
Lemon, 1 TBS.	1/2 tsp. lemon extract.
Cake Flour, 1 C.	1 C. minus 2 TBS. all purpose flour.
Self-rising flour, 1 C.	1 C. all purpose flour, 1/2 tsp. baking soda, 1/2 tsp. baking powder, and 1/2 tsp. lite salt.
Hard Cheese, 1 oz.	1 oz. low-fat cheese, or 2 TBS. grated Parmesan, or 1 oz. low-fat processed cheese.
Sour Cream, 1 C.	1 C. reduced fat sour cream or 1 C low fat cottage cheese.
Whole Milk, 1 C.	Pureed, Non-fat cottage cheese.
Ricotta cheese	1 C. part skim ricotta, or 1 C. regular cottage cheese, or 1 C. low-fat cottage cheese.
Heavy Cream, 1 C.	1 C. half & half or 1 C. evaporated whole milk, or 1 C. evaporated skim milk.
Regular Ice Cream, 1 C.	1 C. ice milk, or 1 C. sherbet, or 1 C. non-fat frozen yogurt.
Cream Cheese, 1 oz.	1 oz. reduced fat cream cheese, or 2 TBS. pureed low-fat cream cheese.
Chocolate, 1 oz.	3 tsp. cocoa powder, plus 2 TBS. diet soft margarine.

SUBSTITUTING FLAVORINGS_____

So your sweet tooth is acting up and you want to bake. Are there substitutes for your favorite sweets? Usually, you can find a lower fat version of most products. If you cannot find a lower fat version, try just cutting back the serving size of the original to satisfy that urge, but still reducing the fat. For example, chocolate is the hardest to duplicate. Sure, carob (a chocolate substitute) is out there, but how many of us like the flavor of carob, when we want REAL chocolate. Some recipes call for particular flavorings that can be found in almost any grocery store. If you'd like more variety in flavorings look in a local cake decorating store, where you will find many more flavors. You can locate one by checking the yellow pages in the phone book under Cake Decorating. The main difference between the flavorings in cake stores and those from supermarkets is that cake store decorating flavors don't have COLOR since colors would add a tint to the frostings.

There are currently new sugar free chocolates made by Van Leer Company. They do have fat, but for the diabetic it's wonderful, and tastes like real chocolate. It comes in Milk Chocolate, White and Semi sweet. Ask your local Cake Decorating shop if they carry it.

*NOTE: If you go this route you must be disciplined enough at this point so you do not go crazy in this kind of store. Almost all items in the cake decorating stores are FATTENING. You can ask if they have a fat free frosting or cake recipes. I'm sure they'd be happy to oblige.

Remember to keep the substitutions as NATURAL as we can. Our bodies really don't like synthetic things.

SPICES AND HERBS_____

A Spice of Life

Learning about spices and herbs will increase the ability to enhance a recipe to your liking, or give it a new twist. This section is a guide to help you to know which spices go with what foods. This guide contains suggestions so you can play with spices and have fun, not rules. When trying new recipes, it is best to stick with the original recipe for the first time, so you can get a feel for what the dish is supposed to taste like.

SPICE:	CAN BE USED IN:
Allspice	Sweet baked goods. Can enhance meat dishes as well. Eggplant, parsnips, spinach, squash and turnips. Curries, rice dishes and puddings.
Basil	Has a little mint flavor, like marjoram. All meat varieties. Asparagus, green beans, squash, tomatoes, and even waxed beans. Popular in Italian cooking. Compliments garlic.
Chili	Best in beef and chicken dishes, also in shrimp. Cauliflower, corn, lima beans, onions and peas. Best known in Mexican dishes. There are many kinds of chili peppers. Most often used as chili powder.
Cinnamon	Enhances pork. Carrots, onions, spinach, squash, sweet potatoes and yams. Baked goods such as cakes, breads and cookies.
Cloves	Beef, chicken and fish dishes. Beets, carrots, onions, squash and sweet potatoes. Used

favorably in sweets, and sauces, fruit and curried dishes.

Cumin   All meat variety dishes especially in Middle East and Mexican dishes. Also good in lamb, curries and yogurt dishes.

Curry   Primarily in Indian and Asian dishes. Can be made mild or hot. All meat variety dishes. Potatoes, carrots, onions, broccoli and cauliflower.

Dill   From the parsley family. Lamb, shellfish, chicken and beef dishes. Cabbage, carrots, cauliflower, peas, potatoes and sauerkraut. Also used in cottage cheese, rice dishes and eggs. Onion rolls, cakes and breads.

Garlic   Good in hot or cold dishes. Good in any meat, fish or poultry dish.

Ginger   Chicken and beef dishes, as well as fish. Beets, carrots, squash and sweet potatoes. Also used in sweets, rice dishes and baked beans.

Mace   Shrimp, chicken, and fish dishes. Broccoli, Brussels sprouts, cabbage and succotash. Also used in chocolate desserts, custards and other sweets.

Marjoram   From the Mint family. Shellfish, chicken and turkey dishes. Also good in all other meat dishes. Celery, greens, potatoes, zucchini, salads and fruit dishes.

Mint   Like peppermint, used in many sweets. Used also in vegetables, peas, carrots and cauliflower.

Nutmeg   Any meat, poultry, or shellfish dish. Eggs and fruit dishes. Celery, eggplant, greens, potatoes, zucchini and fruit dishes. Especially good in milk and cheese dishes.

Oregano   Meat and some chicken dishes. Broccoli, cabbage, mushrooms, onions and tomatoes. Used in Italian and Mexican foods.

Parsley   Distinctive flavor. Usually a food garnish, or after dinner palate cleanser. All meat varieties. Sandwiches, soups, sauces and egg dishes.

Rosemary   Baked goods. Popular in sweets. Good in lamb and pork dishes.

Sage   All meat category dishes. Best with pork and duck. Brussels sprouts, eggplant, lima beans, squash, tomatoes and onion soups. Egg dishes, cheese and cheese dips.

Savory   Just about any dish. Does not mix well in sweets.

Tarragon   Chicken and seafood dishes. Especially good in roasting chicken and egg dishes. Soups and delicate vegetables.

Thyme   Popular in poultry, and all meat varieties. Artichokes, carrots, green beans, mushrooms, peas and potatoes. Egg dishes and some bread products. Stocks, marinades, stuffing, soups and sauces.

Vanilla   From the vanilla bean but usually sold as a liquid. Good in any sweet dish. Adds flavor to chocolate.

NOTES:

SECTION III: RECIPES FOR THE SOUL

COOKBOOK SECTION

*ABBREVIATIONS*_____

TEASPOON	tsp.
TABLESPOON	TBS.
CUP	C.
OUNCE	oz.
CAN	can
PACKET	pkt.
PACKAGE	pkg.
PIECES	pcs.
QUART	qt.
PINT	pt.
POUNDS	lbs.
FLUID OUNCE	fl. oz.
LARGE	lg.
MEDIUM	med.
SMALL	sm.

1

SOUPS AND SALADS

English Clam Chowder

SERVINGS : 8

SERVING SIZE: 1 Cup

13	oz.	Clams, canned
1	C.	Onion, chopped
1	Med.	Garlic clove, minced
3	Med.	Potatoes, raw, peeled, cubed
1/2	tsp.	Thyme, ground
1/4	C.	All purpose flour
4	TBLS.	All purpose flour
2 1/2	C	Skim milk
28	oz.	Clam juice, bottle
	Dash	Pepper
		Non-stick cooking spray

1. Drain clams and reserve liquid. Set clams and liquid aside.

2. Coat a dutch oven with non-stick spray or use a Teflon coated sauce pan. Place over medium heat and add onion and garlic. Saut'e until golden brown.

3. Add reserve clam liquid, potatoes, thyme and clam juice. Bring to a boil over medium heat. Cover and simmer 20 minutes or until potatoes are tender.

4. Place 2 cups potato mixture in blender or food processor and process until smooth. Add potato puree bake to pan, stir well and stir in clams.

5. Place flour and water in a bowl and mix with wire whisk (if no whisk available use covered container and shake). Add to chowder. Cook over medium heat approximately 10 minutes stirring constandtly. Serve with ground pepper.

   * HINT: If you like butter flavor, add a dash of butter substitute to top of chowder before serving.

Nutritional Analysis

Calories	119	6%	Total Fat	.62 g.	1%
Protein	8.7 g.	17%	Cholesterol	12.5 mg.	6%
Carbohydrate	19.6g.	6%	Sodium	334 mg.	10%

Calories from Protein: 29% Carbohydrate: 66% Fat: 5%

Shellfish Chowder

SERVINGS: 8
SERVING SIZE: 1 CUP

PREPARATION TIME: 1 Hour
COOKING TIME: 10 Minutes

1	TBS.	Butter substitute, Butter Buds	2	C	Clam juice
2	C.	Onion, chopped	15	oz.	Peeled tomatoes canned
1	C.	Carrots, diced	3/4	lb.	Shrimp
1	C.	Celery, diced	1/2	lb.	Scallops
2	Med.	Potatoes, peeled and cut in chunks	1/4	C.	All purpose flour
			3	TBS.	All purpose flour
1 1/2	tsp.	Paprika	1/2	C.	Skim milk
3/4	tsp.	Thyme, ground	1/4	C.	Parsley, fresh
1/8	tsp.	Pepper	1/4	C.	Wine, Sherry (optional)
1/2	C.	Water			
1	TBS.	Tomato paste			

1. Add butter substitute, onion, carrots, celery and a little water in a dutch oven or heavy sauce pan. Cover and cook 15 minutes, stirring occasionally.

2. Add potatoes, paprika, thyme, pepper, water, tomato paste, clam juice and tomatoes. Bring to a boil, cover and simmer about 45 minutes.

3. Peel and devein shrimp. (can use frozen and peeled shrimp but changes flavor a little)

4. Place flour in bowl and gradually and milk mixing with a wire whisk. Add to chowder.

5. Cook over medium heat until soup thickens stirring constantly.

6. Add shrimp, scallops, parsley and sherry (optional) and stir. Cook until seafood is done, approximately 5 minutes (shrimp will be very pink and scallops will be very white when cooked).

Nutritional Analysis

Calories	187	9%	Total Fat	1.53 g.	2%
Protein	19.4 g.	38%	Cholesterol	82 mg.	41%
Carbohydrate	26 g.	7%	Sodium	446 mg.	14%

Calories from Protein: 40% Carbohydrate: 53% Fat: 7%

Shrimp and Rice Chowder

SERVINGS: 6
SERVING SIZE: 1 Cup

2	TBS.	Butter substitute, Butter Buds
1	Med.	Onion, chopped
2	Med.	Garlic cloves, chopped
1/2	tsp.	Cumin seed
21.5	oz.	Chicken broth, low sodium, 2 cans
2/3	C.	White rice, long grain, uncooked
3	Med.	Tomatoes, raw, peeled and diced
10	oz.	Peas, frozen
1	lb.	Shrimp
1	Med.	Lime

1. In a large sauce pan combine oil, onion, garlic and cumin. Stir over medium-high heat until onion is limp. Approximately 5 minutes.

2. Add broth and rice. Bring to boil over high heat. Cover and simmer until rice is cooked approximately 30 minutes.

3. Add tomatoes, peas and about 3/4 of the shrimp. Simmer until hot. Place in bowls for serving and add remaining shrimp and a lime wedge for garnish. Paprika can be used as garnish, also.

Nutritional Analysis

Calories	216	11 %	Total Fat	2.87 g.	4 %
Protein	23.6 g.	46 %	Cholesterol	116 mg.	58 %
Carbohydrate	28 g.	8 %	Sodium	242 mg.	7 %

Calories from Protein: 41 % Carbohydrate: 48 % Fat: 11 %

Spicy Fish Chowder

SERVINGS: 6
SERVING SIZE: 1 1/2 Cups

PREPARATION TIME: 30 Minutes
COOKING TIME: 60 Minutes

1	TBS.	Butter substitute, Butter Buds
1	C.	Onion, chopped
1	C.	Carrot, shredded
2	Med.	Potato, peeled, skinned, in chunks
2	TBS.	Tomato paste
1	TBS.	Worcestershire Sauce
3/4	tsp.	Thyme, ground
28	oz. 2 cans	Tomato, low sodium, 2 cans
2	C.	Clam juice
2	Pcs.	Bay leaf
2	lbs.	Halibut
1/4	C.	Parsley, dried
1/2	tsp.	Hot pepper sauce, Tobasco optional

1. Add onion, carrot, and butter substitute in large sauce pan. Sauté for approximately 5 minutes, until onions are limp.

2. Add potatoes, tomato paste, Worcestershire sauce, thyme, hot sauce, tomatoes, bay leaves, and clam juice: Bring to a boil. Cover, reduce heat and simmer for approximately 45 minutes. Potatoes should be tender.

3. Add fish and parsley. Cover and simmer again for about 5 - 10 minutes, until fish is cooked (fish will be very white).

4. Discard bay leaves.

Nutritional Analysis

Calories	253	13 %	Total Fat	4 g.	5 %
Protein	34.4 g.	67 %	Cholesterol	57 mg.	28 %
Carbohydrate	20 g.	6 %	Sodium	352 mg.	11 %

Calories from Protein 54%   Carbohydrate 32%   Fat 14%

Vegetable Clam Chowder

SERVINGS: 8
SERVING SIZE: 1 Cup

PREPARATION TIME: 20 Minutes
COOKING TIME: 20 - 25 Minutes

1	C.	Onion, chopped
1	qt.	Clam broth
1	C.	Water
2	C.	Potatoes, diced
1	C.	Carrots, sliced
1	C.	Celery, diced
9	oz.	Green beans, frozen, (1 pkg.)
1/2	tsp.	Thyme
1/8	tsp.	Pepper
4	C.	Tomatoes, diced
1	tsp.	Parsley
14	oz.	Clams, minced, canned

1. Mix clam broth, water, potatoes, celery, carrots, onions, thyme and pepper.

2. Over moderate heat and bring to boil. Reduce heat and simmer for 20 minutes or until vegetables are tender.

3. Add tomatoes, green beans, parsley and undrained clams. Heat thoroughly.

*HINT: Skim milk may be used instead of water, for a thicker flavor.

Nutritional Analysis

Calories	151	8 %	Total Fat	1.87 g.	2 %
Protein	13 g.	26 %	Cholesterol	13.2 mg.	7 %
Carbohydrate	23 g.	7 %	Sodium	410 mg.	12 %

Calories from Protein: 32 % Carbohydrate: 57 % Fat: 10 %

95

Chicken and Rice Soup

SERVINGS: 7
SERVING SIZE: 1 Cup

PREPARATION TIME: 20 Minutes
COOKING TIME: 35 Minutes

1	C.	Chicken, diced	1/4	C.	Onion, chopped
1/2	C.	White rice, long grain uncooked	2	TBS.	All purpose flour
1	Pkg.	Chicken bouillon	3/4	C	Egg substitute, Egg Beaters
32	oz.	Chicken broth, condensed, low sodium	3	TBS	Lemon juice
			2	TBS.	Parsley, dried
					Dash Pepper
1	Med.	Carrot	1	TBS.	Margarine, imitation, low fat
1	Stalk	Celery			

1. Chop carrots and celery.

2. In large saucepan, combine chicken broth, bouillon, rice, carrots, celery and onion. Bring to a boil, reduce heat. Cover; simmer 20 minutes or until rice and vegetables are tender.

3. Stir in chicken. Remove from heat.

4. In small saucepan, melt margarine. Stir in flour. Cook 1 minute until smooth and bubbly. Stirring constantly.

5. Gradually stir in 2 cups broth mixture; cook until slightly thickened, stirring constantly

6. In small bowl, beat eggs until foamy.

7. Gradually beat in lemon juice and 2 cups thickened broth mixture. Slowly add egg mixture in large saucepan, stirring constantly.

8. Heat gently until soup thickens enough to coat a spoon, stirring frequently. Do not boil Add pepper to taste. Garnish with parsley

Nutritional Analysis

Calories	177	9%	Total Fat	4.8 g.	6%
Protein	16.5g.	32%	Cholesterol	19.7 mg.	10%
Carbohydrate	15.8g.	5%	Sodium	307 mg.	9%

Calories from Protein: 38% Carbohydrate: 37% Fat: 25%

Egg Flower Soup

SERVINGS: 4
SERVING SIZE: 1 Cup

PREPARATION TIME: 15 Minutes
COOKING TIME: 20 Minutes

10.8	oz. Can	Chicken broth, low sodium
1 1/8	C.	Peas, frozen
1/4	C.	Carrots, frozen
1/4	lb.	Shrimp
1/4	tsp.	Pepper
1	tsp.	Salt
2	Lg.	Egg whites
1	TBS.	Cornstarch
1/2	tsp.	Sesame oil

1. Place chicken broth, in sauce pan and heat. Add shrimp, carrots and peas.

2. Heat until a slight boil. Beat eggs and SLOWLY add to boiling mixture. Reduce heat.

3. Add salt, pepper and sesame oil.

4. In a small bowl, place 1 tablespoon cornstarch and a few drops of water to make a thin paste. Mix together.

5. Pour cornstarch mixture into soup and let boil about 1 minute, and serve.

*HINTS:

• Do not let egg boil heavily, as they will become very small pieces, rather than a shredded look.
• If you've never used cornstarch, it will mix like cement at first, until enough water is added to make a paste.

Nutritional Analysis

Calories	82	4 %	Total Fat	1.94 g.	3 %
Protein	11.4 g.	22 %	Cholesterol	44 mg.	22 %
Carbohydrate	5.5 g.	2 %	Sodium	171 mg.	5 %

Calories From Protein: 54% Carbohydrate: 26% Fat: 21%

French onion Soup

5	C.	Beef broth, canned, low sodium
1	tsp.	Butter substitute, Butter Buds (liquid)
4	Med.	Onion
12	tsp.	Sugar substitute, Sweet 'n Low
2	TBS.	All purpose flour
1/2	C.	Wine, white table, or water
1.2	tsp.	Thyme leaves
1	tsp.	Bay leaves
1/4	tsp.	Pepper
1	Med.	Garlic clove
2	TBS	Parmesan, grated

1. Slice the onions and add to saucepan cooking, uncovered, until golden, 9-10 minutes with butter buds.

2. Blend in the sugar and flour and cook stirring about 3 minutes.

3. Add the beef broth, water, thyme, bay leaf, and pepper; raise the heat to moderately high and bring to a boil, stirring constantly, about 6 minutes. Adjust heat so that the mixture slightly bubbles. Simmer for 30 minutes.

Nutritional Analysis

Calories	109	5%	Total Fat	1.55 g.	2%
Protein	6.4g.	13%	Cholesterol	2g.	1%
Carbohydrate	13.6 g.	4%	Sodium	145 mg.	4%

Calories from Protein: 27% Carbohydrate: 58% Fat: 15%

Mama Theresa's Chili

SERVINGS: 8
SERVING SIZE: 1 Cup

PREPARATION TIME: 15 Minutes
COOKING TIME: 45 Minutes

1	lb.	Chicken breast, white meat, ground
1	Med.	Onion
2	TBS.	Chili powder
1	tsp.	Cumin seed
15	oz.	Kidney beans, canned or fresh
8	oz.	Tomato puree
1	C.	Celery, diced
1	tsp.	Pepper
6	fl. oz.	Water

1. In a skillet, sauté ground turkey, onions, salt, pepper, and 1 tablespoon of chili powder.

2. In a large sauce pan add water, tomato sauce, chopped tomatoes, kidney beans, and heat. If using fresh kidney beans, soak overnight, and cook before adding to chili.

3. Add meat mixture to tomato base, add remaining chili powder, and cumin. Heat over medium heat until heated through. for a more flavorful soup, simmer for 1 hour.

*HINTS:

- If more chili flavor is desired, add more chili powder a teaspoon at a time, until flavor is reached.
- If a thicker chili is desired, add a cornstarch and water mixture to the soup while slightly boiling. Make by adding 1 1/2 TBS. cornstarch to 1/4 C. water and mixing to make paste.
- Using dark chicken meat will raise fat content.

Nutritional Analysis

Calories	139	7 %	Total Fat	1.39 g.	2 %
Protein	12.5 g.	25 %	Cholesterol	33 mg.	16 %
Carbohydrate	15.3 g.	4 %	Sodium	266 mg.	8 %

Calories From Protein: 41% Carbohydrate: 49% Fat: 10%

Pea Soup

2	C.	Split peas
5	C.	Water
1	tsp.	Bay leaves, ground
1/2	tsp.	Salt, lite
1	C.	Onion, chopped
1/2	tsp.	Thyme, ground
1/2	tsp.	Pepper
1/2	tsp.	Garlic powder
2	TBS.	Lemon juice or vinegar
2	C.	Carrots, sliced

1. Combine dried split peas, water, bay leaf, and salt substitute in large kettle. Bring to a boil and then reduce heat and simmer for 1 1/2 hours. stir occasionally and check to make sure there is enough water and that the split peas do not stick. Add more water if it becomes too dry.

2. Add carrots, onions and Herb's. Continue to simmer for 30 minutes or longer (overcooking cannot hurt this soup, as long is it is stirred to prevent sticking).

3. Just before serving add the vinegar or lemon juice and more pepper, if desired.

Nutritional Analysis

Calories	43	2 %	Total Fat	0.17 g.	0 %
Protein	2.9 g.	6 %	Cholesterol	0 mg.	0 %
Carbohydrate	8.4 g.	2 %	Sodium	53 mg.	2 %

Calories From Protein: 25% Carbohydrate: 72 % Fat: 3 %

Summer Strawberry Soup

SERVING SIZE: 1 Cup
SERVINGS: 2

PREPARATION TIME: 25 Minutes
COOKING TIME: 30 Minutes

2	C.	Strawberries
1	tsp.	Cornstarch
1 TBS. plus 1/4 C.		Orange juice, concentrate
1/2	C.	Water
1/4	C.	Yogurt, plain, nonfat

1. Clean and cut strawberries into halves. Hold about 5 strawberries off to the side for later use.

2. Using food processor, if available, mash and cut strawberries into a puree.

3. In a saucepan, place 3 tablespoons of orange juice with cornstarch and dissolve cornstarch. After dissolved, add remaining orange juice, water and pureed strawberries. Heat over medium heat. When mixture comes to a boil, remove from heat and cool.

4. Thoroughly mix in yogurt, cover and refrigerate for approximately 4 hours.

5. Place into bowls and cut remaining 5 strawberries into halves lengthwise and place on top of soup and serve.

Nutritional Analysis

Calories	82	4%	Total Fat	.62 g.	1%
Protein	2.54g.	5%	Cholesterol	0g.	0%
Carbohydrate	18 g.	5%	Sodium	24 mg.	1%

Calories from Protein: 12% Carbohydrate: 82%   Fat: 6%

Zucchini Soup

SERVINGS: 9
SERVING SIZE: 1 Cup

PREPARATION TIME: 20 Minutes
COOKING TIME: 30 Minutes

4	C	Zucchini, sliced
1 1/2	oz.	Chicken broth, condensed, low sodium
1/4	C.	Water
1	tsp.	Basil
1/2	tsp.	Pepper
2	C.	Milk, skim
2	TBS.	Cornstarch
1	Med.	Onion
1	Med.	Garlic clove, minced
1	TBS.	Margarine, imitation, low fat

1. In a 5-6 quart kettle, melt margarine over medium heat.

2. Chop onion and add with garlic to margarine and cook. Stirring, until onions are limp (about 5 minutes).

3. Add the zucchini slices, chicken broth, 2 cups of water, basil and pepper.

4. Bring to a boil, reduce heat, cover and simmer until zucchini is very tender (about 20 minutes).

5. In a bowl blend skim milk, 1/4 cup water and cornstarch.

6. Increase heat and add the cornstarch mixture to the kettle and cook, stirring, until soup boils and thickens slightly.

Nutritional Analysis

Calories	62	3%	Total Fat	0.94 g.	1%
Protein	5.8g.	11%	Cholesterol	1.56g.	1%
Carbohydrate	8 g.	2%	Sodium	62 mg.	2%

Calories from Protein: 37% Carbohydrate: 50% Fat: 13%

Egg Salad

SERVINGS: 2
SERVING SIZE: 1/2 Cup

PREPARATION TIME: 25 Minutes
COOKING TIME: 10 Minutes

4	Lg.	Eggs whites
2	C.	Spinach
2	TBS.	Lemon juice
1/2	tsp.	Basil
1/2	tsp.	Garlic powder
1/2	tsp.	Mustard, yellow
2	TBS.	Mayonnaise, fat free

1. Boil eggs to a hard boil. Remove shell, and yolks. Cut into chunks.

2. Add all spices together in a small bowl, with mustard, lemon juice, and non-fat mayonnaise. Stir well, until smooth and creamy.

3. Add eggs and spinach to mixture, and serve. For more flavor, refrigerator for 1 hour.

*HINT: Place egg salad over a green salad mixture. Or, place in large lettuce leaves, and sprinkle with paprika for garnish.

Nutritional Analysis

Calories	93	5 %	Total Fat	0.62 g.	1 %
Protein	12.7 g.	25 %	Cholesterol	0 mg.	0 %
Carbohydrate	11.3 g.	3 %	Sodium	360 mg.	11 %

Calories From Protein: 50 % Carbohydrate: 44 % Fat: 5 %

Heavenly Fruit Salad

SERVINGS: 2
SERVING SIZE: 1 1/2 Cups

PREPARATION TIME: 30
COOKING TIME: 0

1	Med.	Orange
1	Med.	Apple
1	C.	Strawberries
1	Med.	Banana
1	C.	Grapes
1	Med.	Pear
1	TBS.	Lemon juice
1	TBS.	Sugar
1/2	tsp.	Vanilla extract

1. Peel, cut and core all hard fruits. Cut into bite size wedges. Place in a bowl of cold water, and sprinkle with a little salt (the salt prevents fruit from turning brown).

2. Wash and rinse grapes. Take from vine if still attached. Set aside.

3. Drain water from hard fruits, add all fruits together in a large bowl.

4. Add lemon juice, and vanilla, mix well and serve.

*HINT: If a whipped topping mixture is desired on the fruit, omit vanilla, and add the Marshmallow Frosting recipe on page 222.

Nutritional Analysis

Calories	253	13 %	Total Fat	1.56 g.	2 %
Protein	2.5 g.	5 %	Cholesterol	0 mg.	0 %
Carbohydrate	64 g.	18 %	Sodium	7.4 mg.	0 %

Calories From Protein: 4 % Carbohydrate: 91 % Fat: 5 %

Mixed Bean Salad

SERVINGS: 4
SERVING SIZE: 1 Cup

PREPARATION TIME: 20 Minutes
COOKING TIME: 1 Hour

1/2	C.	Kidney beans, dried
1/4	C.	Black beans, dried
1/2	C.	Lima beans, dried
3 3/4	oz.	Garbanzo beans, canned
1/4	C.	Navy beans, dried
1	Med.	Garlic clove, crushed
1/2	TBS.	Parsley, Fresh
1/2	TBS.	Basil
1	TBS	Vinegar
1	Med.	Tomato, raw
1/2	C.	Cucumber, sliced
1/2	C.	Green beans

1. In a large sauce pan, place beans (except for green beans) and water enough to cover beans twice. Boil beans until soft. About 45 minutes to 1 hour.

2. Cut green beans into 1 inch slices, and add to other beans cooking when there is about 15 minutes left remaining on bean mixture time.

3. Remove beans from water and rinse with cold water.

4. In a large bowl, add all ingredients (tomatoes should be last, cutting in small pieces) to beans. Chill and serve. Can be served at room temperature, but refrigerating brings out flavor more.

Calories	127	6%	Total Fat	0.77 g.	1%
Protein	7.9g.	15%	Cholesterol	0g.	0%
Carbohydrate	25 g.	7%	Sodium	257 mg.	8%

Calories from Protein: 23% Carbohydrate: 72% Fat: 5 %

Pasta Tuna Salad

SERVINGS: 2
SERVING SIZE: 1 Cup

4 1/2	oz.	Tuna, packed in water, 1 1/2 cans or 1 6 1/8 oz.
1/2	C.	Peas, frozen
1/2	Med.	Tomato, raw
1/2	C.	Onion, chopped
1/2	TBS.	Dill weed
2	tsp.	Garlic powder
2	tsp.	Oregano
2	tsp.	Thyme, ground
1/2	C.	Yogurt, plain, nonfat
1/2	TBS.	Parsley, dried
1 1/2	C.	Shell macaroni, cooked

1. Cook shell macaroni, and set aside.

2. In a large bowl, mix together all spices, and yogurt.

3. Drain water from tuna. Add tuna and pasta to spice mixture. Mix well. May be served right away, or refrigerated to bring out flavor more.

*HINT: Other pasta's may be used in place of shells, if shells are not available.

Nutritional Analysis

Calories	331	17 %	Total Fat	2.9 g.	4 %
Protein	28.6 g.	56 %	Cholesterol	36 mg.	18 %
Carbohydrate	47 g.	13 %	Sodium	313 mg.	9 %

Calories From Protein: 35 % Carbohydrate: 57 % Fat: 8 %

Spinach/Tomato Salad

SERVINGS: 6
SERVING SIZE: 1 Cup

PREPARATION TIME: 45 Minutes
REFRIGERATION TIME: 1 Hour

10	oz.	Spinach, frozen
7	Med.	Tomato, raw
1/2	C.	Celery
1/2	C.	Onion, chopped
2	TBS.	Vinegar
1	tsp.	Dill weed
1/4	tsp.	Garlic powder
3	TBS.	Mustard, dried
	Dash	Pepper
1 1/2	C.	Rice, white, long grain, cooked

1. In small bowl, combine all dressing ingredients (vinegar, oil, dill weed, salt, garlic powder, mustard, and pepper); mix well.

2. Chop 1 tomato; thaw spinach and squeeze to drain.

3. In medium bowl, combine cooked rice, spinach, tomato, onions and celery; mix well.

4. Pour dressing over salad mixture; toss well. Refrigerate 1 hour to blend flavors.

5. Prepare remaining 6 tomatoes: hollow out stem portion at center of each tomato. Make 6 vertical cuts from top of each tomato to about the middle of the tomato making sure not to cut through bottom. Peel skin back to form a "tulip". Spoon about 2/3 cup salad mixture into each tomato tulip.

Nutritional Analysis

Calories	135	7 %	Total Fat	2.04 g.	3 %
Protein	5.5 g.	11 %	Cholesterol	0 mg.	0 %
Carbohydrate	26 g.	7 %	Sodium	47 mg.	1 %

Calories From Protein: 15% Carbohydrate: 72% Fat: 13%

Super Spinach Greens

SERVINGS: 2
SERVING SIZE: 1 Cup

PREPARATION TIME: 35 Minutes
COOKING TIME: 15 Minutes

1/2	lb.	Chicken, white, ground
1/2	C.	Onion, chopped
1	Med.	Garlic clove, minced
1	C.	Mushrooms, sliced
4	C.	Spinach, 1 cup cooked
1/2	C.	Green pepper, sliced
1/2	C.	Yogurt, plain, low fat
1	oz.	Cottage cheese, low fat 1%
1	tsp.	Oregano
1	TBS.	Butter substitute, Butter Buds

1. Sauté turkey, onion, green pepper and garlic in a skillet until slightly brown and tender.

2. Rinse spinach off, and cut half of stem off.

3. Place about a 1/4 cup water in skillet, add spinach and mushrooms. Cook until spinach becomes limp. The add remaining ingredients, non-fat yogurt, cottage cheese and oregano. Heat and serve.

Nutritional Analysis

Calories	376	19 %	Total Fat	4 g.	5 %
Protein	35 g.	69 %	Cholesterol	70 mg.	35 %
Carbohydrate	47 g.	13 %	Sodium	538 mg.	16 %

Calories From Protein: 38 % Carbohydrate: 52 % Fat: 10 %

Veggie Salad

1	C.	Broccoli
1	C.	Cauliflower
1/2	Med.	Green pepper
1	Med.	Cucumber
3	Med.	Carrot
2	Med.	Tomato, raw
1/2	C.	Italian dressing, low calorie

1. Break broccoli and cauliflower into florets.

2. Cut green pepper into 1" squares.

3. Slice cucumber.

4. Pare and slice carrots.

5. Combine vegetables; toss with dressing, cover and refrigerate 1 hour. Better if it can be refrigerated overnight.

Nutritional Analysis

Calories	68	3%	Total Fat	3 g.	4%
Protein	1.9g.	4%	Cholesterol	0g.	0%
Carbohydrate	9.9 g.	3%	Sodium	329 mg.	10%

Calories from Protein: 10% Carbohydrate: 53% Fat: 37%

Yogurt Coleslaw

SERVINGS: 4
SERVING SIZE: 1 Cup

PREPARATION TIME: 2 Hours
COOKING TIME: 0

3	TBS.	Yogurt, plain, nonfat
3/4	tsp.	Mustard, yellow
1.2	tsp.	Sugar
1/2	tsp.	Vinegar
1/4	tsp.	Celery seed
	Dash	Pepper
1 3/4	C.	Cabbage
1/4	C.	Carrot, shredded

1. In a medium-size bowl, combine the yogurt, sour cream, mustard, sugar, vinegar, celery seeds, salt and pepper.

2. Coarsely shred the cabbage and add with carrot; toss well to mix. Cover and chill in the refrigerator for 2 to 3 hours, tossing occasionally.

Nutritional Analysis

Calories	18.7	1%	Total Fat	0.11 g.	0%
Protein	1 g.	2%	Cholesterol	0g.	0%
Carbohydrate	3.8 g.	1%	Sodium	27 mg.	1%

Calories from Protein: 20% Carbohydrate: 75% Fat: 5%

2

POULTRY

Barbecued Turkey Breast

SERVINGS: 10   PREPARATION TIME: 15 Minutes
SERVING SIZE: 1/2 Pound   COOKING TIME: 1 Hour and 15 Minutes

5	lb.	Turkey, 1/2 Breast, skinned
1/2	C.	Ketchup, low sodium
1	TBS.	Water
1	TBS.	Sugar, brown, low calorie
1 1/2	tsp.	Worcestershire Sauce
1	tsp.	Mustard, yellow

1. Prepare charcoal fire for grilling.

2. Rinse turkey breast; pat dry.

3. In small bowl prepare sauce. Combine ketchup, brown sugar, water, Worcestershire sauce and mustard.

4. Place turkey breast on grill 4 to 6 inches from medium coals; cover or use aluminum foil "tent".

5. Cook 1 to 1 1/2 hour or until juices are no longer pink when pierced with fork, turning turkey once halfway through cooking . Brush with sauce last 5 minutes of cooking.

Nutritional Analysis

Calories	262	13%	Total Fat	1.57 g.	2%
Protein	55 g.	109%	Cholesterol	141g.	70%
Carbohydrate	2.66 g.	1%	Sodium	214 mg.	6%

Calories from Protein: 90% Carbohydrate: 4 % Fat: 6%

Meat Loaf

SERVINGS: 4
SERVING SIZE: 1 Serving

PREPARATION TIME: 20 Minutes
COOKING TIME: 1 Hour

1	lb.	Turkey, white, ground
15	fl. oz.	Tomato puree
1/4	C.	Water
2	TBS.	Mustard, yellow
1	TBS.	Vinegar
3	oz.	Cheerios, crushed
3	Lg.	Egg whites
1	Med.	Onion
1/4	tsp.	Pepper

Preheat oven to 350 °.

1. Combine tomato sauce, water, mustard and vinegar.

2. Mix ground turkey with Cheerio crumbs, egg white, chopped onion, pepper and 1/4 of the tomato sauce mixture. Shape into a loaf.

3. Place into a bread loaf pan.

4. Pour enough sauce over top of meat loaf to coat. Bake at 350 ° for 1 hour, basting often. Extra sauce may be warmed and served over sliced meat loaf.

Nutritional Analysis

Calories	285	14 %	Total Fat	2.26 g.	3 %
Protein	36 g.	70 %	Cholesterol	70 mg.	35 %
Carbohydrate	28.4 g.	8 %	Sodium	436 mg.	13 %

Calories From Protein: 52% Carbohydrate: 41% Fat: 7%

Mushroom Burger

SERVINGS: 2
SERVING SIZE: 1 Pattie

PREPARATION TIME: 15 Minutes
COOKING TIME: 15 Minutes

1/2	lb.	Turkey, 1/2 breast, ground
1/2	C.	Mushrooms, sliced
1/2	C.	Onion, sliced
1	Med.	Hamburger bun
2	Lg.	Egg whites
2	oz.	Cheerios
	Dash	Pepper
	Dash	Salt
		Non-stick cooking spray

1. Cut onions and mushrooms into thin slices.

2. Place onions and mushrooms into a skillet, with a little non stick spray, (or liquid Butter Buds may be substituted, if a butter flavor is desired). Brown, remove from heat, and set aside.

3. Mix turkey with egg whites, Cheerios (crushed to a cracker dust), salt and pepper together. Mix well.

4. Divide into 2 patties (1/4 pound each), and place in a skillet with a little non-stick spray. Cook until done.

5. Place a little of the mushroom/onion mixture on the hamburger and heat thoroughly. Remove and serve.

*HINT: Broiling may be done in place of using a skillet.

Nutritional Analysis

Calories	335	17%	Total Fat	3.7 g.	5%
Protein	37.4 g.	73%	Cholesterol	71g.	35%
Carbohydrate	33g.	9%	Sodium	1451 mg.	44%

Calories from Protein: 47% Carbohydrate: 4 2% Fat: 10%

Nachos

1	lb.	Turkey, 1/2 breast, skinned
1/2	tsp.	Coriander, ground
1	TBS.	Chili powder
3/4	tsp.	Cumin seed
1/4	tsp.	Pepper
6 oz.	Can	Tomato paste, low salt
1/2	C.	Water
6		Tortilla, corn
1	C.	Refried beans
1	C.	Cheddar cheese, low fat
1/2	C.	Sour cream, low fat, (optional)
		Salsa, (optional)

Preheat oven to 325 °.

1. Brown turkey and drain. Add spices, tomato paste and water (tomato sauce can be substituted, add a 15 ounce can of sauce and NO water). Lower heat to simmer, and simmer for about 5 minutes.

2. On a pizza pan, spread a thin layer of refried beans. Add meat on top of beans.

3. Grate cheese, and sprinkle over top of meat. Place in oven at 325 ° and melt cheese, about 5 minutes.

4. Remove from oven, and top with low fat sour cream, (salsa, and diced tomatoes are optional). Sprinkle chips around pizza tray on a larger pizza pan, or serve chips in a bowl. Dip chips into nacho mixture.

*HINTS:
- Chips can be placed on pizza pan, omitting refried beans, placing instead all ingredients on top of chips, and heating.
- You can add store-bought salsa or use the salsa recipe in sauce and dip section.

Nutritional Analysis

Calories	437	22 %	Total Fat	11.7 g.	15 %
Protein	43 g.	84 %	Cholesterol	113 mg.	56 %
Carbohydrate	38.5 g.	11 %	Sodium	1062 mg.	32 %

Calories From Protein: 40% Carbohydrate: 36% Fat: 24%

Pigs n' The Blanket

SERVINGS: 4
SERVING SIZE: 2 Rolls

PREPARATION TIME: 45 minutes
COOKING TIME: 60 minutes

8	Leaves	Cabbage
1/2	C.	Rice, white, long grain, uncooked
1 1/2	C.	Tomato puree
1/2	lb.	Turkey, ground
1/2	C.	Onion, chopped
	Dash	Pepper
	Dash	Salt, lite
1/2	C.	Water

Preheat oven to 350 °.

1. Separate cabbage leaves and place leaves in warm water to soften, while preparing rest of ingredients.

2. Mix meat, rice, onion, salt and pepper together.

3. Remove cabbage from water. Take a small ball of meat mixture, and place in center of cabbage leaf, roll cabbage until leaf covers meat. Fold in ends, and place a toothpick through, to hold all together.

4. In a baking dish (such as a casserole dish), place cabbage balls in dish, and pour water and tomato sauce over the top, making a soupy sauce.

5. Bake in oven at 350 degrees for 30 minutes. Reduce heat to 325 degrees and bake an additional 30 minutes.

Nutritional Analysis

Calories	251	13 %	Total Fat	7.2 g.	10 %
Protein	16 g.	32 %	Cholesterol	48 mg.	24 %
Carbohydrate	29.6 g.	8 %	Sodium	112 mg.	3 %

Calories from Protein: 26 % Carbohydrate: 48 % Fat: 26 %

Tacos

SERVINGS: 4
SERVING SIZE: 2 Each

PREPARATION TIME: 25 Minutes
COOKING TIME: 30 Minutes

1	lb.	Turkey, ground
1	TBS.	Chili powder
3/4	tsp.	Cumin powder
1/2	tsp.	Coriander, ground
1/4	tsp.	Pepper
3	C.	Lettuce, shredded
1	Med.	Tomato, raw
8	Pcs.	Taco shells
9	oz. Can	Tomato sauce, low salt
1/2	C.	Water
1	oz.	Cheddar cheese, low fat

1. Brown ground turkey, drain off excess fat. Add spices and tomato sauce. Reduce heat to simmer and simmer for approximately 5 minutes.

2. Slice lettuce into thin shreds.

3. Dice tomatoes into small bite size pieces.

4. Place in separate bowls, and serve on table family style or make tacos ahead and serve.

5. Taco shells or tortillas may be heated slightly.

*HINT: Packaged taco spices can be substituted, but the sodium content will be raised.

Nutritional Analysis

Calories	311	16 %	Total Fat	6.8 g.	9 %
Protein	35 g.	68 %	Cholesterol	75 mg.	38 %
Carbohydrate	31.4 g.	9 %	Sodium	200 mg.	6 %

Calories From Protein: 43% Carbohydrate: 39% Fat: 19%

Turkey Burger

SERVINGS: 4
SERVING SIZE: 1 Pattie

PREPARATION TIME: 15 Minutes
COOKING TIME: 15 Minutes

1	lb.	Turkey, white, ground
1	Pkt.	Lipton Dry Onion Soup
2	Lg.	Eggs whites
2	oz.	Cheerios
4	Med.	Hamburger bun

1. In a plastic bag, place Cheerios, and crush with a rolling pin until a cracker crumb consistency is acquired.

2. In a large bowl, add all ingredients and mix well with hands or fork.

3. Divide into 4 1/4 pound patties, and cook in a broiler pan or skillet, until meat is thoroughly brown.

*HINT: If only 1 or 2 patties are desired, make others into patties and freeze for another time.

Nutritional Analysis

Calories	309	15 %	Total Fat	3.54 g.	5 %
Protein	34.5 g.	68 %	Cholesterol	71 mg.	35 %
Carbohydrate	30 g.	9 %	Sodium	628 mg.	19 %

Calories From Protein: 48% Carbohydrate: 42% Fat: 11%

Turkey Stuffed Eggplant

SERVINGS: 8
SERVING SIZE: 1/2 Eggplant Each

4	Med.	Eggplant
2	Med.	Onion
42	oz.	Tomato, canned, crushed
2	lb.	Turkey, white, ground
1	TBS.	Parsley, dried
1/2	tsp.	Salt, lite
1/2	tsp.	Pepper
1/4	C.	Water

Preheat oven to 350 °.

1. Remove stems from eggplants; cut in half lengthwise and remove pulp leaving 1/2 inch thick shell. Arrange halves in baking dish.

2. Chop pulp.

3. Chop onion and sauté with ground turkey. Add water and chopped pulp for 15 minutes or until vegetables are tender.

4. Add tomatoes, parsley, salt and pepper.

5. Spoon mixture into eggplant halves; cover. Bake at 350 ° for 45 minutes or until done.

Nutritional Analysis

Calories	202	10 %	Total Fat	1.1 g.	1 %
Protein	30 g.	58 %	Cholesterol	70 mg.	35 %
Carbohydrate	17.3 g.	5 %	Sodium	172 mg.	5 %

Calories From Protein: 60% Carbohydrate: 35% Fat: 5%

Turkey, Yam and Pineapple Skewers

SERVINGS: 4
SERVING SIZE: 1 Skewer

PREPARATION TIME: 25 Minutes
COOKING TIME: 50 Minutes

4	Med.	Sweet potatoes or yams
8.3	oz.	Pineapple, light syrup, canned
1/4	C.	Water
12	C.	Cranberry sauce
10.3	oz.	Turkey, 1/2 breast, skinless
		Bamboo skewers

SAUCE:

2	TBS.	Brown Sugar, low calorie
1	tsp.	Cornstarch
1/2	tsp.	Cinnamon
1/4	tsp.	Mustard, dried
	Dash	Cloves, ground

1. In a saucepan cook yams or sweet potatoes in enough boiling salted water to cover, for 25 to 30 minutes or until just tender. Drain; cool.

2. Peel and cut into 1-inch chunks.

3. Drain pineapple slices, reserving 1/3 cup of the syrup. Quarter each pineapple slice.

4. For sauce: in a small sauce pan stir together brown sugar, cornstarch, cinnamon, mustard and cloves.

5. Stir in the reserved pineapple syrup and cranberry sauce. Cook and stir until slightly thickened and bubbly. Cook and stir 1 to 2 minutes more.

6. Cut turkey breast into 12 pieces. On 4 skewers, thread turkey pieces, sweet potato or yams and pineapple pieces.

7. Place the skewers on an unheated rack 5 to 6 inches from heat. Broil 4 minutes brushing occasionally with sauce. Turn skewers and broil about 4 minutes more brushing with sauce. A barbecue may be used instead of broiling.

Nutritional Analysis

Calories	305	15%	Total Fat	0.81 g.	1%
Protein	20 g.	40%	Cholesterol	46g.	23%
Carbohydrate	55g.	16%	Sodium	62 mg.	2%

Calories from Protein: 26% Carbohydrate: 71% Fat: 2%

Chicken & Egg Over Rice

SERVINGS: 2
SERVING SIZE: 1 1/2 Cups

10.4	oz.	Chicken breast, skinless
1	C.	Egg substitute
1/2	Med.	Onion
4	Med.	Mushroom, Shitake or Asian
1	Pcs.	Green onion
2	C.	Rice, white, short grain, cooked

SAUCE:

1/2	C.	Water
6	TBS.	Soy Sauce, low sodium
6	TBS.	Mirin
2	TBS.	Sugar

1. Cut chicken breasts into bite size chunks.

2. Place Shitake mushrooms in water to soak. Place a heavy object on mushrooms to sink mushrooms into water. Soak about 15 minutes.

3. Cut onion in half width-wise. Using half of onion, cut into thin slices, and cut thin slices in half once again width-wise.

4. Mix sauce ingredients in a small sauce pan, and simmer until sugar is dissolved.

5. Take half of sauce and place in small skillet sauce pan. Add chicken and onion. Boil over medium high heat until chicken is almost done.

6. Remove mushrooms from water and cut off hard stem. Cut mushrooms into quarters, and set aside.

7. Cut green onion into small pieces.

8. Beat 2 eggs in a small bowl, and place half of mushrooms with eggs. Mix together. Pour over chicken mixture, and cover. Poach until the egg mixture looks semi hard.

9. Place as much rice as desired in the bottom of a deep bowl, and gently place chicken mixture over rice, pouring also sauce.

Nutritional Analysis

Calories	557	28 %	Total Fat	6.7 g.	9 %
Protein	50 g.	97 %	Cholesterol	85 mg.	43 %
Carbohydrate	60 g.	17 %	Sodium	554 mg.	17 %

Calories From Protein: 40 % Carbohydrate: 48 % Fat: 12 %

Chicken And Veggie Chow Mien

SERVINGS: 4
SERVING SIZE: 3/4 Cup

PREPARATION TIME: 25 Minutes
COOKING TIME: 15 Minutes

1/2	lb.	Chicken Breast, skinless
2	C.	Noodles, cooked
1 1/2	TBS.	Soy Sauce, low sodium
1	TBS.	Sugar, chopped
1/2	Med.	Carrot, cut in thin strips
1	Med.	Garlic clove, chopped
1	Med.	Onion, halved and cut in thin strips
5	Med.	Mushrooms, chopped
1/3	C.	Egg substitute, Egg Beaters

SAUCE:

2	TBS.	Soy Sauce, low sodium
1	TBS.	Sugar
1	TBS.	Green onion, chopped
1	Med.	Garlic clove
1	TBS.	Sesame oil
1/4	tsp.	Pepper

1. Cut chicken into thin strips, let stand in marinating sauce.

2. Cut carrots into thin strips and sauté lightly.

3. Cut onion in half, and then into thin slices, and add to carrots, in pan.

4. Boil noodles in water until soft. Rinse under cold water to prevent sticking. Cut noodles with knife or scissors into 8 - 10" lengths.

5. Add chicken and mushrooms to carrots and onions and sprinkle with sugar and soy sauce.

6. Combine all other ingredients to chicken mixture and stir fry until heated through.

*HINTS:
- When cooking Chinese style, always start with light colored vegetables first. Fry the meat, and dried mushrooms last.
- Allowing Chicken to marinate overnight produces a better flavor.

Nutritional Analysis

Calories	261	13 %	Total Fat	5.7 g.	7 %
Protein	15.5 g.	30 %	Cholesterol	33 mg.	16 %
Carbohydrate	32 g.	9 %	Sodium	129 mg.	4 %

Calories From Protein: 40 % Carbohydrate: 48 % Fat: 12 %

Chicken Veggie Melody

SERVINGS: 2
SERVING SIZE: 1 Cup

PREPARATION TIME: 20 Minutes
COOKING TIME: 15 Minutes

1/4	lb.	Chicken breast, skinless
1/2	Med.	Onion
1/2	Med.	Green pepper
1	Med.	Zucchini
1/2	C.	Mushrooms, sliced
8	oz.	Tomato, canned, peeled
1	Med.	Garlic clove, minced
1/2	tsp.	Oregano
1.2	tsp.	Basil
1/2	C.	Water

1. Cut onions and chicken into thin slices, place in a skillet and brown. (Add small amount of water to prevent meat from sticking).

2. Slice all vegetables into chunks or slices, and add all remaining ingredients to the meat and chicken in the skillet.

3. Bring to a slight boil and reduce heat. Summer until vegetables are soft. Serve hot.

   * (HINT: If a thicker sauce is desired add a cornstarch and water mixture to vegetable mixture while slightly boiling. Add 1 1/2 TBS. cornstarch to 1/4 c. water, mixing to make a paste.)

Nutritional Analysis

Calories	118	6%	Total Fat	1.35 g.	2%
Protein	11.3 g.	22%	Cholesterol	33g.	16%
Carbohydrate	12g.	3%	Sodium	265 mg.	8%

Calories from Protein: 43% Carbohydrate: 4 6% Fat: 12%

Mark's Simple Chicken

SERVINGS: 2
SERVING SIZE: 1 Breast

PREPARATION TIME: 10 Minutes
COOKING TIME: 20 Minutes

| 2 | 8 oz. | Chicken Breast, skinless |
| 3/4 | C. | Salsa |

1. Using a small cake pan or shallow cooking pan.

2. Turn oven on to broil, place oven rack on 2nd or 3rd shelf.

3. Place chicken breasts side by side in pan, pouring salsa over chicken to cover.

4. Place in oven. Cook until half cooked, turn chicken over when salsa has a dried look, or approximately 20 minutes. Cook underside of chicken until done.

*HINT: If a store bought salsa is not available, use homemade. Recipe is in the sauce and dip section.

Nutritional Analysis

Calories	154	8 %	Total Fat	1.4 g.	2 %
Protein	16.8 g.	33 %	Cholesterol	66 mg.	33 %
Carbohydrate	6 g.	2 %	Sodium	733 mg.	22 %

Calories From Protein: 65% Carbohydrate: 23% Fat: 12%

Porcupine Balls

1	lb.	Chicken, ground
1/2	C.	Rice, uncooked
1	C.	Water
3	TBS.	Onion, chopped
26	oz.	Tomatoes, diced (1 can) or Tomato soup
2	TBS.	Worcestershire sauce
1/2	tsp.	Garlic powder
	Dash	Pepper

1. In a large bowl, mix rice, chicken, onion, garlic, and pepper.

2. Form into medium sized meatballs.

3. Place in skillet . Add tomatoes, water, and Worcestershire sauce. Cover and simmer 1 hour over low heat.

Nutritional Analysis

Calories	401	20 %	Total Fat	14.4 g.	19 %
Protein	32 g.	62 %	Cholesterol	95 mg.	48 %
Carbohydrate	36 g.	10 %	Sodium	166 mg.	5 %

Calories from Protein: 32 % Carbohydrate: 36 % Fat: 32 %

Sesame Yogurt Chicken

SERVINGS: 4
SERVING SIZE: 1 1/2 Cups

PREPARATION TIME: 30 Minutes
COOKING TIME: 1 Hour

1	C.	Yogurt, plain, nonfat
2	TBS.	Honey
4	oz.	Corn Flakes
1/4	tsp.	Ginger, ground
3/4	tsp.	Paprika
	Dash	Cayenne pepper
2	lb.	Chicken, whole fryers, skinless
1/4	C.	Butter substitute, Butter Buds
	Dash	Pepper

Prepare oven to 350°.

1. Cut up chicken into pieces.

2. Combine honey and yogurt.

3. In another bowl combine corn flake crumbs, ginger, paprika and pepper.

4. Dip chicken pieces in yogurt mixture and roll in crumb mixture until well coated.

5. Place in single layer on a large, greased baking pan.

6. Sprinkle butter substitute, on top of chicken. Bake at 350° for 1 hour or until chicken is tender. Do not cover or turn chicken during baking.

Nutritional Analysis

Calories	342	17%	Total Fat	5.7 g.	8%
Protein	42.5 g.	83%	Cholesterol	94g.	47%
Carbohydrate	25g.	7%	Sodium	348 mg.	11%

Calories from Protein: 53% Carbohydrate: 31% Fat: 16%

3

SEAFOOD

Deviled Crab

SERVINGS: 4
SERVING SIZE: 1/4 Cup

PREPARATION TIME: 25 Minutes
COOKING TIME: 25 Minutes

1	lb.	Crab Meat	1	tsp.	Lemon juice
3		Green onions		Dash	Cayenne pepper
3	TBS.	All purpose flour	1	oz.	Cheerios
2/3	C.	Milk, skim	1	TBS.	Parsley, dried
2	tsp.	Mustard, brown	4	tsp.	Lemon peel
6	TBS.	Butter substitute, liquid, Butter Buds			

Preheat broiler.

1. Finely chop green onion.

2. In a medium-size heavy saucepan, over moderate heat; add the scallions and 2 TBS. butter substitute, Butter Buds, and cook until just tender (about 5 minutes).

3. Blend in the flour and cook 3 minutes more.

4. Add the milk and cook, stirring constantly, until the mixture is thick and smooth, about 5 minutes.

5. Remove from heat and mix in mustard, lemon juice and cayenne pepper. Stir in the crab meat and parsley; set aside.

6. Melt the remaining butter substitute (4 TBS.), Butter Buds, in a small saucepan over moderate heat, stir in the bread crumbs, and set aside.

7. Spoon equal amounts of the crab mixture into 4 lightly greased scallop shells or individual baking dishes. Sprinkle with equal amounts of the crumb mixture.

8. Broil 7 to 9 inches from the heat until browned, about 3 to 4 minutes. Garnish with strips of lemon peel.

Nutritional Analysis

Calories	179	9 %	Total Fat	2.1 g.	3 %
Protein	26.4 g.	52 %	Cholesterol	101 mg.	51 %
Carbohydrate	9.7 g.	3 %	Sodium	506 mg.	15 %

Calories From Protein: 65% Carbohydrate: 24% Fat: 12%

Foiled Again Fish

SERVINGS: 2
SERVING SIZE: 8 Ounces

1	lb.	Halibut
8	Slices	Tomato
1	Pc.	Green onion
1/2	tsp.	Dill weed
1	tsp.	Pepper
1/4	C.	Water

Pre-heat oven to 400 °.

1. Place half of fish in center of a piece of foil. Fold edges slightly up. Make two of these.

2. Top fish with tomato slices, green onion and zucchini.

3. Sprinkle with herbs. Sprinkle water over the fish to keep it moist. Fold edges up further and crimp at the top to close foil (making a tent).

4. Bake for approximately 10 - 15 minutes or until flaky.

Nutritional Analysis

Calories	260	13 %	Total Fat	5.3 g.	7 %
Protein	47 g.	93 %	Cholesterol	72 mg.	36 %
Carbohydrate	3.3 g.	1 %	Sodium	128 mg.	4 %

Calories from Protein: 76 % Carbohydrate: 5 % Fat: 19 %

Hawaiian Shrimp & Scallop Skewers

SERVINGS: 4
SERVING SIZE: 1 Skewer

PREPARATION TIME: 30 Minutes
COOKING TIME: 10 Minutes

1/2	lb.	Scallops
1/2	lb.	Shrimp
1 1/2	C.	Pineapple, diced
8	Med.	Mushrooms
1/2	Med.	Red pepper
1/2	Med.	Onion
2	TBS.	Lemon juice

1. Place scallops, shrimp, pineapple, mushrooms, and lemon juice all together, and let sit 10 minutes.

2. Remove and reserve any juice from above items, set aside for later. Begin to skewer all vegetables, and seafood in an alternate pattern.

3. When all skewers are done, either barbecue or broil skewers, about 2 - 3 minutes on each side. Baste with left over juice while cooking.

*HINTS:

- Can be served over rice.

- If you try to replace any vegetable with a harder vegetable, remember: Cooking seafood only takes a few minutes, therefore, hard vegetables may not be cooked thoroughly.

Nutritional Analysis

Calories	148	7 %	Total Fat	1.9 g.	2 %
Protein	22.3 g.	44 %	Cholesterol	106 mg.	53 %
Carbohydrate	12.7 g.	4 %	Sodium	181 mg.	5 %

Calories From Protein: 57% Carbohydrate: 32% Fat: 11%

133

Lemon Peppered Barbequed Cod

SERVINGS: 2   PREPARATION TIME: 1 Hour and 15 Minutes
SERVING SIZE: 1 Fillet   COOKING TIME: 10 Minutes

1	lb.	Cod
1	Med.	Lemon Juice
1	tsp.	Onion, chopped
1/2	tsp.	Oregano
1/2	tsp.	Paprika
1/2	tsp.	Basil
1/4	tsp.	Pepper

1. Combine juice of lemon, chopped onions, oregano, paprika and basil. Add cod and marinate in refrigerator for about 1 hour.

2. Place foil on grill (or in oven on broiler pan) and grill for about 10 minutes or until flaky.

3. Garnish with either a lemon peel or orange and serve.

Nutritional Analysis

Calories	196	10%	Total Fat	1.77 g.	2%
Protein	40.5 g.	79%	Cholesterol	97g.	48%
Carbohydrate	3.8g.	1%	Sodium	136 mg.	4%

Calories from Protein: 84% Carbohydrate: 8% Fat: 8%

Orange Roughy And Tomatoes

SERVINGS: 2   PREPARATION TIME: 25 Minutes
SERVING SIZE: 5 Ounces   COOKING TIME: 30 Minutes

10	oz.	Orange Roughy or Bass
1/4	C.	Onion, chopped
1	Med.	Garlic clove, minced
1/2	tsp.	Butter substitute, liquid, Butter Buds
1	Med.	Tomato, raw
	Dash	Oregano
	Dash	Thyme, ground
	Dash	Pepper
1/4	C.	Water
1 1/2	tsp.	Tomato paste

Preheat over to 350 °.

1. Chop and seed tomato.

2. In oven-proof skillet over medium heat, sauté onion and garlic in liquid butter substitute, Butter Buds, until soft, about 5 minutes.

3. Stir in tomato and seasonings. Cover and simmer for 5 minutes.

4. Place fish in skillet; cover with sauce. pour water over fish. cover and bake for 15-20 minutes or until fish flakes with fork.

5. Remove fish to heated platter.

6. Reduce sauce on top of range to 1/3 cup.

7. Stir in tomato paste and pour over fish. Serve with lemon wedges.

Nutritional Analysis

Calories	177	9 %	Total Fat	4.7 g.	6 %
Protein	26.5 g.	52 %	Cholesterol	72 mg.	36 %
Carbohydrate	6.4 g.	2 %	Sodium	494 mg.	15 %

Calories From Protein: 61% Carbohydrate: 15% Fat: 25%

Scallops ala Marinade (Skewers)

SERVINGS: 4
SERVING SIZE: 1 Skewer

PREPARATION TIME: 2 Hours
COOKING TIME: 5 Minutes

1	lb.	Scallops
1	Med.	Zucchini
1	Med.	Red onion
2	TBS.	Lemon juice
2	TBS.	Parsley, dried
1/2	tsp.	Fennel seed
1	Med.	Garlic clove, minced
1	TBS.	Orange rind
1/8	C.	Cooking wine
		Metal or bamboo skewers

Preheat broiler.

1. In a medium-size bowl, whisk together cooking wine, lemon juice, parsley, fennel seeds, garlic, and orange rind. Add the scallops and toss well; cover and refrigerate at least 1 - 2 hours. The longer the marinade process the more flavor.

2. Slice zucchini into 1/4 inch slices; quarter onion and cut into small wedges.

3. Thread scallops onto 4 lightly greased, long metal skewers, alternating with the zucchini and onion.

4. Lay the skewers on the broiler pan rack and broil 4 to 5 inches from the heat, turning once or twice, until the scallops are pure white. Transfer to heated dinner plates.

Nutritional Analysis

Calories	131	7 %	Total Fat	0.98 g.	1 %
Protein	20 g.	39 %	Cholesterol	38 mg.	19 %
Carbohydrate	7.6 g.	2 %	Sodium	191 mg.	6 %

Calories From Protein: 67% Carbohydrate: 25% Fat: 7%

Shrimp Creole

1	lb.	Shrimp, shelled and deveined
1	Med.	Garlic clove
1	Stalk	Celery
1/2	Med.	Green pepper
2 1/2	C.	Onion, chopped
3 or 4	C.	Tomato puree
1	tsp.	Bay leaves, ground
1	tsp.	Basil
1/4	tsp.	Pepper
	Dash	Hot pepper sauce
	Dash	Worcestershire sauce
1	Pkt.	Chicken bouillon
1/2	tsp.	Sugar
1/4	C.	Parsley, fresh
		Non-stick cooking spray

1. Add onions, minced garlic clove, diced green pepper and cut celery in diagonal strips; sauté, using non-stick cooking spray, until limp and golden.

2. Add tomato sauce, bay leaf, basil, pepper, hot pepper sauce, Worcestershire sauce, chicken bouillon, chopped parsley and sugar; simmer, partially covered, for 1 hour.

3. Add shrimp (shelled and deveined); cook 2 to 3 minutes, stirring constantly, until shrimp are pink and firm. Serve over rice.

Nutritional Analysis

Calories	170	8 %	Total Fat	1.8 g.	2 %
Protein	19.5 g.	38 %	Cholesterol	116 mg.	58 %
Carbohydrate	25 g.	7 %	Sodium	352 mg.	11 %

Calories From Protein: 40% Carbohydrate: 51% Fat: 8%

Shrimp Stir Fry

SERVINGS: 2   PREPARATION TIME: 15 Minutes
SERVING SIZE: 1 Cup   COOKING TIME: 10 - 15 Minutes

1/2	lb.	Shrimp
1/2	10 oz. Pkg.	Mixed vegetables, frozen
1	Med.	Garlic clove, minced
2	TBS.	Soy Sauce, low sodium
1/2	tsp.	Ginger, ground
1	TBS.	Sugar

1. If shrimp is still in shell, clean, devein and remove tails.

2. In a skillet, place shrimp, garlic, and ginger, and sauté lightly over medium high heat.

3. Add remaining ingredients, and constantly stirring cook until shrimp is thoroughly cooked, and vegetables are heated through.

*HINT: If individual vegetables are desired, replace mixed vegetables with 1/8 cup of each.

Nutritional Analysis

Calories	215	11 %	Total Fat	2.5 g.	3%
Protein	28 g.	55 %	Cholesterol	173 mg.	86 %
Carbohydrate	23.6 g.	7 %	Sodium	294 mg.	9 %

Calories From Protein: 49% Carbohydrate: 41% Fat: 10%

Stuffed Halibut

SERVINGS: 4
SERVING SIZE: 1 Piece

PREPARATION TIME: 35 Minutes
COOKING TIME: 40 Minutes

1	lb.	Halibut
2 TBS. plus 1/4 C.		Butter substitute, liquid, Butter Buds
1/4	C.	All purpose flour
2		Bay leaves
1/4	C.	Milk, skim
1/4	C.	Water
1/2	C.	Rice, wild or short grain white, cooked
1 1/2	C.	Rice, white, long grain, cooked
1/4	C.	Parsley, dried
2	TBS.	Parsley, dried
1	tsp.	Lemon juice

Preheat oven to 375 °.

1. Mix and measure 2 TBS. butter substitute, Butter Buds, and combine with basil and thyme.

2. Heat milk and stir in gradually. Stir in water and cook, stirring until smooth and thick.

3. Combine wild and brown rice and 1/4 cup parsley; add to sauce and toss lightly to combine.

4. Slice each fillet down the side seam to form a pocket; spoon in rice mixture.

5. Secure with toothpicks if necessary. Place on oiled baking pan.

6. Mix 1/4 cup Butter Buds with 1 1/2 tablespoons parsley flakes and lemon juice; brush on fillets. Bake at 375 ° for 40 minutes or until done. Garnish with lemon slices.

Nutritional Analysis

Calories	328	16 %	Total Fat	3.34 g.	4 %
Protein	30 g.	59 %	Cholesterol	37 mg.	19 %
Carbohydrate	36 g.	10 %	Sodium	108 mg.	3 %

Calories From Protein: 41% Carbohydrate: 49% Fat: 10%

Tuna'd Peppers

SERVINGS: 2
SERVING SIZE: 1/2 Pepper

6 1/2	oz	Albacore Tuna
2	TBS.	Onion, chopped
2	Med.	Green peppers
2	TBS.	Celery, diced
2	Lrg.	Eggs whites
1/2	tsp.	Dill weed
1/2	tsp.	Fennel seed

Pre-heat oven to 350 °.

1. Cut green pepper horizontally in half. Place bottom half on a cookie sheet.

2. Combine all ingredients and stuff into bottom of pepper halves.

3. Bake for approximately 10 minutes.

Nutritional Analysis

Calories	205	10 %	Total Fat	8.5 g.	11 %
Protein	27 g.	53 %	Cholesterol	32.5 mg.	16 %
Carbohydrate	5.8 g.	2 %	Sodium	66 mg.	2 %

Calories from Protein: 52 % Carbohydrate: 11 % Fat: 37 %

4

BEEF

Beef Stew

SERVINGS: 2
SERVING SIZE: 1 1/2 Cups

PREPARATION TIME: 30 Minutes
COOKING TIME: 30 Minutes

1/2	lb.	Sirloin steak, lean
1	tsp.	All purpose flour
	Dash	Pepper
1/2	C.	Onion, chopped
1	Med.	Garlic clove, minced
1/4	C.	Water
1	C.	Tomato Puree
1	tsp.	Parsley, fresh
1	Pc.	Bay leaf
1	C.	Carrots, chopped
2	Med.	Potato, raw without skin
1/2	C.	Corn
1/2	C.	Peas

1. Cut sirloin steak into chunks.

2. Mix flour and pepper together and roll meat to lightly coat. Brown in skillet for about 10 minutes.

3. In large sauce pan, combine garlic, onion and a little water; brown, for about 3 minutes.

4. Add browned meat to sauce pan, and all other ingredients.

5. Cook until potatoes and carrots are soft, about 30-45 minutes.

6. Mix a little flour and water together for a thickening agent. Add to stew while stew is boiling, and stir constantly until stew thickens.

* TIP: It's possible to substitute Lipton's Onion Soup for onions, to give more flavor. Just add 1 cup more water. Remember, changing this will alter nutrition.

Nutritional Analysis

Calories	440	22%	Total Fat	8.9 g.	12%
Protein	34.4 g.	67%	Cholesterol	73g.	37%
Carbohydrate	60g.	17%	Sodium	121 mg.	4%

Calories from Protein: 30% Carbohydrate: 53% Fat: 17%

Beef Stroganoff

SERVINGS: 4   PREPARATION TIME: 20 Minutes
SERVING SIZE: 4 Cups   COOKING TIME: 25 Minutes

1	lb.	Roast beef, top round, lean
2	TBS.	Flour, all purpose
1	tsp.	Paprika
1	Med.	Onion
1	Med.	Garlic clove
2	TBS.	Water
4	oz.	Mushrooms, sliced to make 1 Cup
1	C.	Yogurt, plain, nonfat
1	Cube	Beef bouillon

1. Slice beef in thin, diagonal strips (may be easier to do if partially frozen).

2. Mix flour and paprika in plastic bag. Add beef strips to bag and shake to coat.

3. Chop onion and cook with water, beef, and garlic over high heat until soft. Stir in mushrooms (undrained if canned), yogurt and bouillon. Heat to boiling, stirring constantly.

4. Reduce heat, cover and simmer for 12-15 minutes. Serve over noodles.

Nutritional Analysis

Calories	219	11 %	Total Fat	5.6 g.	7 %
Protein	30 g.	58 %	Cholesterol	70 mg.	35 %
Carbohydrate	10.2 g.	3 %	Sodium	348 mg.	11 %

Calories From protein: 57% Carbohydrate: 19% Fat: 24%

Green Peppered Steaks

SERVINGS: 2
SERVING SIZE: 5 Ounces

PREPARATION TIME: 15 Minutes
COOKING TIME: 30 Minutes

5	oz.	Sirloin steak, lean
1/2	Med.	Onion
1	Med.	Garlic clove
1/4	tsp.	Oregano
1/4	tsp.	Thyme, ground
1	C.	Green pepper, sliced
1 1/2	tsp.	Cornstarch
		Water
		Non-Stick Cooking Spray

1. Cut onion in half, and cut slices from ends of onions.

2. Cut green pepper in half, clean out seeds, and chop into small pieces. (can slice if it's your preference).

3. Lightly spray skillet with cooking spray. Add meat, onions, and garlic, and brown.

4. Mix together cornstarch and water to make the thickener. mix into meat and onions, stirring constantly until thickened. Add oregano, thyme, and chopped peppers.

5. Cover and let simmer for approximately 15 minutes. More water may be added to thin the sauce or keep from sticking to pan.

Nutritional Analysis

Calories	301	15 %	Total Fat	5.4 g.	7 %
Protein	19 g.	37 %	Cholesterol	46 mg.	23 %
Carbohydrate	45 g.	13 %	Sodium	55 mg.	2 %

Calories From Protein: 25% Carbohydrate; 59% Fat: 16%

Korean Barbecue Beef Marinade

SERVINGS: 4
SERVING SIZE: 3 Ribs

PREPARATION TIME: 2 Hours and 20 Minutes
COOKING TIME: 20 Minutes

1 1/2	lb.	Roast beef, top round, lean
6	TBS.	Sugar
2	TBS.	Mirin, sweet rice wine
1/2	C.	Green onions, chopped
4	Med.	Garlic cloves, minced
6	TBS.	Soy sauce, low sodium
2	TBS.	Sesame oil
1/4	tsp.	Pepper

1. Slice meat into large thin strips, (looking like a circle) about 1/4" thick.

2. Place 3 tablespoons sugar and meat in large bowl and mix well.

3. In separate bowl, mix remaining 3 tablespoons of sugar with remaining ingredients and mix until sugar is dissolved. Add to meat.

4. Marinate meat at least 2 hours. Best if marinated overnight.

* HINT: Mirin may be found in Oriental section of your grocery store or for a lower price at any Oriental grocery store.

Nutritional Analysis

Calories	371	19%	Total Fat	14.8 g.	19%
Protein	42 g.	82%	Cholesterol	105g.	52%
Carbohydrate	13.5g.	4%	Sodium	190 mg.	6%

Calories from Protein: 47% Carbohydrate: 15% Fat: 38%

'Shroom'd Steaks

SERVINGS: 2
SERVING SIZE: 6 Ounces

PREPARATION TIME: 15 Minutes
COOKING TIME: 15 Minutes

1/2	C.	Onion, sliced
3/4	lb.	Roast sirloin tip, lean
1/4	C.	Mushrooms, sliced
	Dash	Pepper
2	TBS.	Butter substitute, liquid, Butter Buds

Preheat oven to broil.

1. Season steaks with pepper (and other spices if desired).

2. Place in oven and cook to desired redness.

3. While steaks are cooking, in a sauté pan, place liquid butter substitute (Butter Buds), onions and mushrooms. Sauté until brown over medium heat.

4. Remove steaks from oven, place onto a plate and pour onions and mushrooms over top and serve hot.

Nutritional Analysis

Calories	231	12 %	Total Fat	7.3 g.	10 %
Protein	32 g.	63 %	Cholesterol	88 mg.	44 %
Carbohydrate	10 g.	3 %	Sodium	278 mg.	8 %

Calories from Protein: 55 % Carbohydrate: 17 % Fat: 28 %

Sir Steaks

SERVINGS: 2
SERVING SIZE: 5 Ounces

PREPARATION TIME: 15 Minutes
COOKING TIME: 15 - 20 Minutes

1/2	C.	Onion, sliced
10	oz.	Roast sirloin tip, lean
1	Med.	Tomato
2	tsp.	Basil
4	TBS.	Water

1. Place steak in non stick skillet or spray skillet with a non fat spray.

2. Add onions and brown approximately 10 minutes over medium heat. Place a small amount of water in the pan to keep meat from sticking.

3. Add tomatoes, basil and cover. Cook to desired doneness.

4. May garnish with parsley and serve.

Nutritional Analysis

Calories	221	11 %	Total Fat	7.2 g.	9 %
Protein	31.4 g.	62 %	Cholesterol	85 mg.	42 %
Carbohydrate	7 g.	2 %	Sodium	58 mg.	2 %

Calories from Protein: 58 %   Carbohydrate: 13 %   Fat: 30 %

5

GRAINS

Buckwheat Pancakes

SERVINGS: 8
SERVING SIZE: 1 Piece (4" Diameter)

PREPARATION TIME: 15 Minutes
COOKING TIME: 5 - 8 Minutes

3/4 - 1	C.	Flour, whole wheat
1	tsp.	Sweet 'n Low
2	tsp.	Baking powder
2	Lg.	Egg white
1	TBS.	Butter substitute
1 1/2	C.	Milk, skim
	Dash	Salt (Optional)

1. Stir together flours, brown sugar, baking powder and dash of salt, if desired.

2. Combine egg, milk, and oil. Add this mixture to the flour mixture, stirring until blended but still slightly lumpy.

3. Pour about 1/4 cup batter onto hot lightly greased griddle or heavy skillet.

4. Cook till golden brown, turning to cook other side when pancakes have a bubbly surface and slightly dry edges.

Nutritional Analysis

Calories	70	3 %	Total Fat	.30 g.	0 %
Protein	4.1 g.	8 %	Cholesterol	.63 mg.	1 %
Carbohydrate	13.5 g.	4 %	Sodium	205 mg.	6 %

Calories from Protein: 22 % Carbohydrate: 74 % Fat: 4 %:

Cheese Pizza Crust

SERVINGS: 1
SERVING SIZE: 1 Medium (12 inch)

PREPARATION TIME: 1 Hour
COOKING TIME: 45 Minutes

3 3/4	C.	Flour, all purpose
1	TBS.	Butter substitute
1	oz.	Yeast, active (1 pkt.)
1	tsp.	Salt (optional)
1	C.	Water
1/2	tsp.	Sugar substitute
1/4	C.	Cheese, Parmesan grated

1. Mix in a large bowl, flour, yeast, salt (optional), and sugar substitute.

2. Mix water into above ingredients. Water should be warm (between 105 ° and 115 °).

3. Add to dry ingredients and cheese.

4. Knead by hand for about 5 minutes, or until soft and elastic. Place in bowl, cover and let rise in a warm, draft free place. Rise until double in size. About 30 minutes

5. Punch down. Place onto a lightly floured surface, and roll to desired size.

6. Lightly brush liquid butter substitute onto pizza pan, or cookie sheet. Place dough on top of pan. Let rise again about 15 minutes. Add toppings.

Nutritional Analysis

Calories	1716	86 %	Total Fat	10.1 g.	13 %
Protein	56 g.	110 %	Cholesterol	15 mg.	8 %
Carbohydrate	342 g.	98 %	Sodium	2922 mg.	89 %

Calories from Protein: 13 % Carbohydrate: 81% Fat: 5 %

Cinnamon Rolls

SERVINGS: 8
SERVING SIZE: 1 Roll

PREPARATION TIME: 2 1/2 hrs.
COOKING TIME: 20 - 30 Minutes

4 1/2	C.	Flour, all purpose
1	pkt.	Yeast, active
1	C.	Milk, skim
1/3	C.	Sugar
3/4	C.	Sugar, brown
2-3	TBS.	Cinnamon

6	Lg.	Egg Whites
1/4	C.	Flour, all purpose
1/2	C.	Butter substitute (or applesauce)
1/2	C.	Raisins

1. Mix 2 1/4 cup flour and yeast together.

2. Heat milk, 1/3 cup butter substitute, and 1/3 cup sugar until warm.

3. Add egg whites to milk mixture.

4. Beat for 30 seconds at low speed. Then beat 3 minutes at high speed.

5. Add remaining 2 1/4 cup flour.

6. Turn out and knead until soft and smooth, almost like elastic. (approximately 3-5 minutes)

7. Place in a low fat greased bowl, and turn once. Cover and let rise, about 1 hour or until double in size.

8. Mix filling: combine brown sugar, 1/4 cup flour, cinnamon, and rest of butter substitute. Mix until crumbly.

9. Punch down dough; turn onto floured board. Cover for 10 minutes. Then roll dough in a 12" square.

10. Sprinkle filling over square and top with raisins.

11. Roll dough up, and pinch ends to seal. Slice into 8, 1 1/2" pieces. Set on greased pan (a pizza pan works well) or a 13x9x2" pan.

12. Cover dough loosely with clear plastic wrap. Cover loosely and let rise in a warm area about 45 minutes and then refrigerate for about 2 hours. If baking immediately, don't chill.

13. To bake: Uncover and let stand for 30 minutes. Preheat oven to 375°.

14. Break surface bubbles with a greased toothpick. Bake at 375° for 20-30 minutes or until brown. If not done, and too brown, cover with foil for the remaining 5-10 minutes.

Nutritional Analysis

Calories	406	20 %	Total Fat	0.93 g.	1 %
Protein	11.5 g.	23 %	Cholesterol	0.5 mg.	0 %
Carbohydrate	83 g.	24 %	Sodium	67 mg.	2 %

Calories from Protein: 12%   Carbohydrate: 86%   Fat: 2%

153

Corn Bread

SERVINGS: 15
SERVING SIZE: 1/ 1" Slice

PREPARATION TIME: 20 Minutes
COOKING TIME: 1 Hour and 40 Minutes

1/2	C.	Milk, skim
3	TBS.	Sugar
1/4	C.	Water
1/4	C.	Butter substitute, liquid, Butter Buds
1	Pkg.	Yeast
2	Lg.	Egg whites
1 3/4	C.	Flour, all purpose
3/4	C.	Cornmeal

1. Combine sugar, milk, salt and butter substitute (Butter Buds). Cool to lukewarm.

2. Combine yeast and water; stir until dissolved.

3. In separate bowl, beat egg whites and stir in flour and corn meal.

4. Add in milk mixture and beat 2 minutes or until well blended. (Batter will be stiff).

5. Turn into greased loaf pan (s).

6. Cover; let rise 1 hour or until doubled in bulk. Bake at 375° for 30-35 minutes.

Nutritional Analysis

Calories	77	4%	Total Fat	0.21 g.	0%
Protein	2.5 g.	5%	Cholesterol	0.13g.	0%
Carbohydrate	14.8g.	4%	Sodium	28 mg.	1%

Calories from Protein: 14% Carbohydrate: 83% Fat: 3%

Corny Pizza Crust

SERVINGS: 1
SERVING SIZE: 1 Slice

PREPARATION TIME: 40 Minutes
RISING TIME: 1 Hour and 15 Minutes

1	oz.	Yeast, active (1 pkt.)
3/4	C.	Water
3	tsp.	Sugar or Sugar substitute
1 1/3	C.	Flour, all purpose
1/2 C. +		
1 TBS.		Cornmeal
1/4	tsp.	Salt, lite (optional)
1/2	tsp.	Butter substitute

1. Mix yeast into warm water and dissolve. Add sugar to yeast and water.

2. Mix 1 1/3 cups of flour, 1/2 cup cornmeal, and salt (optional). Pour yeast mixture into dry ingredients. Mix well.

3. Place dough on lightly floured surface, knead in a rolling motion, until it becomes smooth, and elastic. (If dough begins to stick to surface, add a little flour).

4. Place dough in a large bowl. (a non stick spray can be sprayed on bowl to prevent sticking).

5. Cover and let stand for approximately 45 minutes, in a warm, draft free space.

6. When dough has doubled in size, punch down. Place on a floured surface again, and roll into a 12" circle. Sprinkle Pizza pan or cookie sheet with, left over cornmeal. Place 12" round on pizza pan.

7. Cover and let stand for about 30 minutes, in a warm, draft free place.

Nutritional Analysis

Calories	826	41 %	Total Fat	2 g.	3 %
Protein	23.7 g.	46 %	Cholesterol	0 mg.	0 %
Carbohydrate	174 g.	50 %	Sodium	492 mg.	15 %

Calories from Protein: 12 % Carbohydrate: 86 % Fat: 2 %

Dinner Rolls

SERVINGS: 16
SERVING SIZE: 1 Roll

PREPARATION TIME: 7 Hours
COOKING TIME: 20-30 Minutes

2 3/4	C.	Flour, all purpose 2		2	Lg.	Egg whites
1/3	C.	Oats, dry		3/4	C.	Flour, whole wheat
1/4	C.	Sugar		1	TBS.	Water
1	Pkg.	Yeast, active		1	TBS.	Oats, dry
1	C.	Milk, skim		1/4	C.	Egg substitute,
3	TBS.	Butter substitute liquid, Butter Buds				Egg Beaters

Grease a 9-inch square pan.

1. In large bowl, combine 1 cup all purpose flour, 1/3 cup rolled oats, sugar, and yeast, blend well.

2. In a pan, heat milk and butter substitute until very warm, 120°-130°.

3. Add warm liquid and 2 egg whites to flour mixture.

4. Blend at low speed until moistened; beat 2 minutes at medium speed.

5. By hand, stir in whole wheat flour and additional 1/2 to 1 1/4 cups all purpose flour until dough pulls cleanly away from sides of bowl.

6. On floured surface, knead in 1/4 to 1/2 cup all purpose flour until dough is smooth and elastic, about 5 minutes.

7. Place dough in greased bowl; cover loosely with plastic wrap and cloth towel. Let rise in warm place (80°-85°) until light and doubled in size, about 1 hour.

8. Punch down dough several times to remove all air bubbles.

9. Divide into 16 equal pieces; shape into balls. Place in prepared pan.

10. Cover; let rise in warm place until light and doubled in size, about 35 to 45 minutes. Heat oven to 375°.

11. In a small bowl, combine egg substitute and water; beat slightly.

12. Carefully brush over rolls; sprinkle with 1 tablespoon rolled oats.

13. Bake at 375° F for 20 to 30 minutes or until golden brown.

14. Remove from pan immediately; serve warm.

Nutritional Analysis

Calories	124	6%	Total Fat	0.46 g.	1%
Protein	4.5 g.	9%	Cholesterol	0.25g.	0%
Carbohydrate	24.4g.	7%	Sodium	19.5 mg.	1%

Calories from Protein: 15% Carbohydrate: 82% Fat: 3%

Garlic Pizza Crust

SERVINGS: 1
SERVING SIZE: 1 Medium (12 inch)

PREPARATION TIME: 1 Hour
COOKING TIME: 45 Minutes

3 3/4	C.	Flour, all purpose
1	TBS.	Butter substitute
1	oz.	Yeast, active (1 pkt.)
1	tsp.	Salt
1	C.	Water
1/2	tsp.	Sugar substitute
2	Med.	Garlic clove, minced

1. Mix in a large bowl, flour, yeast, salt (optional), and sugar substitute.

2. Mix water into above ingredients. Water should be warm (between 105 ° and 115 °).

3. Add to dry ingredients and garlic.

4. Knead by hand for about 5 minutes, or until soft and elastic. Place in bowl, cover and let rise in a warm, draft free place. Rise until double in size. About 30 minutes

5. Punch down. Place onto a lightly floured surface, and roll to desired size.

6. Lightly brush liquid butter substitute onto pizza pan, or cookie sheet. Place dough on top of pan. Let rise again about 15 minutes. Add toppings.

Nutritional Analysis

Calories	1634	82 %	Total Fat	4.3 g.	6 %
Protein	49 g.	95 %	Cholesterol	0 mg.	0 %
Carbohydrate	344 g.	98 %	Sodium	2552 mg.	77 %

Calories from Protein: 12 % Carbohydrate: 86% Fat: 2 %

Oat Bran Muffins

SERVINGS: 12
SERVING SIZE: 1 Muffin

PREPARATION TIME: 20 Minutes
COOKING TIME: 18 - 20 Minutes

2	C.	Flour, whole wheat
1 1/2	C.	Oatmeal, dry
1	tsp.	Ginger
2	tsp.	Cinnamon
3	tsp.	Baking powder
3	pkt.	Sweet 'n Low or 1 cup sugar
1/2	C.	Sugar
2/3	C.	Yogurt, plain, low fat
2	C.	Milk, skim

Pre-heat oven to 350 °.

1. In large bowl, combine flour, oatmeal, ginger, cinnamon and baking powder.

2. Stir in sugars, yogurt and milk.

3. Bake approximately 18 minutes or until toothpick comes out clean.

Nutritional Analysis

Calories	210	11 %	Total Fat	1.62 g.	2 %
Protein	7.3 g.	14 %	Cholesterol	1.44 mg.	1 %
Carbohydrate	44 g.	13 %	Sodium	138 mg.	4 %

Calories from Protein: 13 %   Carbohydrate: 80 %   Fat: 7 %

Poppy Seed Muffins

SERVINGS: 12   PREPARATION TIME: 30 Minutes
SERVING SIZE: 1 Muffin   COOKING TIME: 30 Minutes

3	C.	Flour, all purpose
2 1/4	C.	Sugar, (or sugar substitute)
1 1/2	tsp.	Baking powder
1 1/2	C.	Butter substitute
1 1/2	C.	Milk, skim
6	Lg.	Egg white (or 3/4 cup egg substitute)
1/2	tsp.	Almond extract
1 1/2	TBS.	Poppy seeds

Preheat oven to 350 °.

1. Combine flour, sugar, and baking powder.

2. Whisk butter substitute, milk, egg whites, and Almond extract together,
   until smooth.

3. Add dry ingredients, and mix only until moistened.

4. Stir in poppy seeds.

5. Pour into greased muffin baking tins. Baking papers may be used
   instead of greasing tins.

6. Bake until golden brown. About 30 minutes or until a toothpick inserted
   comes out clean.

Nutritional Analysis

Calories	301	15 %	Total Fat	0.75 g.	1 %
Protein	5.9 g.	12 %	Cholesterol	0.5 mg.	0 %
Carbohydrate	60 g.	17 %	Sodium	98 mg.	3 %

Calories from Protein: 9 %   Carbohydrate: 89 % Fat: 3%

Pumpkin Bread

SERVINGS: 2
SERVING SIZE: 1/2 Slice

PREPARATION TIME: 20 Minutes
COOKING TIME: 60 Minutes

2	C.	Sugar
9	pkt.	Sweet 'n Low
4	Lg.	Egg whites
4	tsp.	Cinnamon
2	tsp.	Nutmeg
2	tsp.	Baking soda
2	C.	Pumpkin, canned
1	C.	Butter substitute, liquid (Butter Buds)
1/2	tsp.	Salt, lite (optional) omitting drops sodium level)

Pre-heat oven to 350 °.

1. Coat two 9 x 5" loaf pans with non stick spray.

2. In a large mixing bowl, mix sugar and liquid butter substitute.

3. Add egg whites and beat well.

4. In another bowl, combine flour, cinnamon, nutmeg, baking soda and salt.

5. Add flour mixture and mix well.

6. Add pumpkin and raisins.

7. Batter may be a little thin.

8. Divide the batter evenly between the two prepared pans. Place in the oven and bake approximately 1 hour or until toothpick comes out clean. Makes 2 loaves.

Nutritional Analysis

Calories	479	24 %	Total Fat	1 g.	5 %
Protein	7 g.	14 %	Cholesterol	0 mg.	0 %
Carbohydrate	105 g.	30 %	Sodium	255 mg.	8 %

Calories From Protein: 6 % Carbohydrate: 92 % Fat: 2 %

Regular Pizza Crust

SERVINGS: 1
SERVING SIZE: 1 Medium (12 inch)

PREPARATION TIME: 1 Hour
COOKING TIME: 45 Minutes

3 3/4	C.	Flour, All purpose
1	TBS.	Butter substitute
1	oz.	Yeast, active (1 pkt.)
1	tsp.	Salt (optional)
1	C.	Water
1/2	tsp.	Sugar substitute

1. Mix in a large bowl, flour, yeast, salt (optional), and sugar substitute.

2. Mix water into above ingredients. Water should be warm (between 105 ° and 115 °).

3. Add to dry ingredients.

4. Knead by hand for about 5 minutes, or until soft and elastic. Place in bowl, cover and let rise in a warm, draft free place. Rise until double in size. About 30 minutes

5. Punch down. Place onto a lightly floured surface, and roll to desired size.

6. Lightly brush liquid butter substitute onto pizza pan, or cookie sheet. Place dough on top of pan. Let rise again about 15 minutes. Add toppings.

Nutritional Analysis

Calories	1624	81 %	Total Fat	4.1 g.	5 %
Protein	48 g.	94 %	Cholesterol	0 mg.	0 %
Carbohydrate	342 g.	98 %	Sodium	2550 mg.	77 %

Calories from Protein: 12 % Carbohydrate: 86 % Fat: 2 %

Whole Wheat Pizza Crust

SERVINGS: 1
SERVING SIZE: 1 Medium (12 inch)

PREPARATION TIME: 1 Hour
COOKING TIME: 45 Minutes

3 3/4	C.	Flour, whole wheat
1	TBS.	Butter substitute
1	oz.	Yeast, active (1 pkt.)
1	tsp.	Salt (optional)
1	C.	Water
1/2	tsp.	Sugar substitute
1/4	C.	Parmesan cheese, grated

1. Mix in a large bowl, flour, yeast, salt (optional), and sugar substitute.

2. Mix water into above ingredients. Water should be warm (between 105 ° and 115 °).

3. Add to dry ingredients.

4. Knead by hand for about 5 minutes, or until soft and elastic. Place in bowl, cover and let rise in a warm, draft free place. Rise until double in size. About 30 minutes

5. Punch down. Place onto a lightly floured surface, and roll to desired size.

6. Lightly brush liquid butter substitute onto pizza pan, or cookie sheet. Place dough on top of pan. Let rise again about 15 minutes. Add toppings.

Nutritional Analysis

Calories	1484	74 %	Total Fat	5.4 g.	7 %
Protein	52 g.	102 %	Cholesterol	0 mg.	0 %
Carbohydrate	314 g.	90 %	Sodium	2553 mg.	77 %

Calories from Protein: 14 % Carbohydrate: 83% Fat: 3 %

6

PASTA AND RICE

Curried Rice

SERVINGS: 2
SERVING SIZE: 1 Cup

PREPARATION TIME: 20 Minutes
COOKING TIME: 30-45 Minutes

2	C.	Rice, white, short grain, uncooked
1/2	C.	Onion, chopped
1	Med.	Garlic clove, minced
1/2	C.	Peas
1/2	C.	Carrots sliced
1	tsp.	Curry powder
2	C.	Water

1. In a large sauce pan (or rice cooker) place all ingredients.

2. Cook for approximately 30 minutes or until rice is a soft texture.

*HINT: If a drier rice is desired, use already cooked rice, and place all ingredients in a saute' pan lightly sprayed with a non-stick spray. Constantly stir, until ingredients are mixed and until rice is warmed through.

Nutritional Analysis

Calories	124	6%	Total Fat	0.46 g.	1%
Protein	4.5 g.	9%	Cholesterol	0.25g.	0%
Carbohydrate	134.4g.	38%	Sodium	34.5 mg.	1%

Calories from Protein: 16% Carbohydrate: 81% Fat: 3%

Oriental Fried Rice

SERVINGS: 4
SERVING SIZE: 1 Cup

PREPARATION TIME: 25 Minutes
COOKING TIME: 30 Minutes

1 1/2	C.	Rice, white, short or long grain, uncooked
1 1/2	TBS.	Soy sauce, low sodium
3	tsp.	Butter substitute
1	Lg.	Egg white
1	C.	Peas
1/4	lb.	Chicken thigh, boneless, skinless
1/4	lb.	Shrimp
1/2	C.	Carrot, shredded
1/2	tsp.	Garlic powder
1/2	C.	Onion, sliced

1. Place rice and 1 1/4 cups water into a pan and cook, covered, over medium heat. Keep covered while cooking, for about 20 minutes or until rice is soft and fluffy. Rice will be slightly dry. If a rice cooker is available, cook according to directions.

2. While rice is cooking, in a large fry pan or wok place chicken, onion and garlic powder, with a little butter substitute to eliminate sticking.

3. Brown, and then add all other ingredients. Stir and mix will.

4. When rice is done, combine everything in frying pan and mix. Cook until rice is browned and ingredients are mixed into rice.

*NOTE: A little more soy sauce may be added in the final step, but be careful as soy sauce has a heavy flavor. Only a little amount at a time should be added.

Nutritional Analysis

Calories	334	17 %	Total Fat	2.4 g.	3 %
Protein	24 g.	48 %	Cholesterol	67 mg.	33 %
Carbohydrate	57 g.	16 %	Sodium	177 mg.	5 %

Calories from Protein: 28 % Carbohydrate : 66 % Fat: 6 %

Spanish Rice

SERVINGS: 2
SERVING SIZE: 1 Cup

PREPARATION TIME: 30 Minutes
COOKING TIME: 30-45 Minutes

2	C.	Rice, white, short grain, cooked
1/4	C.	Green pepper, diced
1/4	C.	Onion, chopped
1/4	C.	Tomato paste
1/2	tsp.	Chili powder
	Dash	Pepper
	Dash	Cumin powder

1. Heat a large saute' pan over high heat, lightly coated with a low-fat no stick spray. Add onions and brown.

2. Place all other ingredients into pan, reduce heat, and constantly stir to eliminate stick-ing. Heat rice and stir until all ingredients are mixed well.

* SHORT CUT TIP: To use uncooked rice, use 1 cup rice to 1 cup water. Cover and boil rice with all ingredients, until rice is cooked.

Nutritional Analysis

Calories	264	13%	Total Fat	.99 g.	1%
Protein	9.5 g.	19%	Cholesterol	0mg.	0%
Carbohydrate	56g.	16%	Sodium	43 mg.	1%

Calories from Protein: 14% Carbohydrate: 83% Fat: 3%

Spinach Lasagna

SERVINGS: 6
SERVING SIZE: 1 - 2" Square

PREPARATION TIME: 40 Minutes
COOKING TIME: 1 Hour

6	oz.	Tomato paste, canned	1/2	C.	Cottage cheese, low fat, 1 %
24	oz.	Tomatoes, canned			
3	Med.	Garlic cloves, minced	1/2	C.	Mushrooms, sliced
1	Med.	Onion, chopped	10	oz.	Spinach, frozen, or 1 lb. fresh
3/4	lb.	Lasagna noodles, uncooked			
			6	oz.	Mozzarella cheese, part skim
1/2	C.	Ricotta cheese, skim milk			
			Dash		Basil
1/2	C.	Parmesan, grated, low fat	Dash		Oregano
			Dash		Rosemary

Preheat oven to 350 °.

1. Sauté onions, and garlic in a low fat non-stick spray.

2. Add tomatoes, tomato paste, and herbs. Simmer for 1/2 hour or longer.

3. Cook noodles in boiling water until tender, and drain.

4. Mix ricotta, parmesan cheese, cottage cheese, and mushrooms. Blend well

5. Steam spinach if using fresh and drain. Or unthaw frozen spinach and set aside.

6. Spread a small amount of sauce on the bottom of a 9 x 13" or 8 x 12" casserole type dish (if not available, a cake pan works well).

7. Place a layer of noodles over the sauce.

8. Spread 1/3 of the cheese mixture over the noodles.

9. Spoon a layer of sauce over the spinach.

10. Repeat layers (noodles, cheese, spinach, sauce) until all ingredients are used. Try to end with noodles and then sauce if you get mixed up.

11. Place thinly sliced mozzarella cheese on top of casserole and bake for about 40 minutes or until bubbly.

Nutritional Analysis

Calories	413	21 %	Total Fat	10.4 g.	14 %
Protein	22.6 g.	44 %	Cholesterol	24 mg.	12 %
Carbohydrate	58 g.	17 %	Sodium	530 mg.	16 %

Calories from Protein: 22 % Carbohydrate: 56 % Fat: 23 %

7

VEGETABLE DISHES

Browned Yams

SERVINGS: 2
SERVING SIZE: 1 Cup

PREPARATION TIME: 15 Minutes
COOKING TIME: 1 Hour

2	C.	Yams
5	TBS.	Sugar, brown
		Water

1. Bake or boil yams until soft.

Preheat oven to 300 °.

2. Peel yams and slice into about 1" slices.

3. Place in a baking dish or bread pan. Add just enough water so yams do not stick.

4. Sprinkle brown sugar over the top of yams and cover with tin foil, making a tent. Place in oven for about 15 minutes at 300 °, or until brown sugar has melted.

*HINT: Marshmallows may be added for extra flavor and color. Place on top just before removing yams from the oven. Remove tinfoil, place in oven on broil. Broil until the marshmallows are brown. Remember, adding marshmallows will change the nutritional analysis.

Nutritional Analysis

Calories	288	14 %	Total Fat	0.2 g.	0 %
Protein	2 g.	4 %	Cholesterol	0 mg.	0 %
Carbohydrate	71 g.	20 %	Sodium	22.4 mg.	1 %

Calories From Protein: 3% Carbohydrate: 97% Fat: 1%

Eggplant and Cheese Casserole

SERVINGS: 4
SERVING SIZE: 2" X 2" Square

PREPARATION TIME: 25 Minutes
COOKING TIME: 1 Hour

2	TBS.	Lemon juice	2	oz.	Cheerios
1	Med.	Eggplant	1/4	C.	Parmesan cheese, grated
16	oz.	Tomato, canned, low sodium	1/2	C.	Cottage cheese, 1 % low fat
16	oz.	Tomato puree			
2	Med.	Garlic cloves	1/4	C.	Mozzarella, part skim milk
1/4	tsp.	Oregano			
1/4	tsp.	Basil			

Preheat broiler.

1. Halve eggplant and slice into 1/4 inch thick slices.

2. Brush eggplant with lemon juice and arrange in a single layer on a non-stick baking sheet; broil 5-6 inches from heat for 2 1/2 minutes on each side or until golden brown.

3. Reduce oven temperature to 350 °, and lower rack.

4. Drain and chop tomatoes. In a medium-size bowl, mix tomatoes with tomato sauce, garlic, oregano, and basil.

5. In a small bowl, combine Cheerios crumbs and Parmesan cheese.

6. Spoon 1/3 of the tomato sauce mixture into a deep 1 1/2 quart casserole, sprinkle with 1/3 of the bread crumb mixture, and cover with a layer of eggplant.

7. Spread 1/2 of the cottage cheese over the eggplant and continue to layer in the same order; ending with the tomato sauce.

8. Scatter the mozzarella cheese over the top and bake for 45 minutes or until bubbling.

9. Increase the heat to broil and place the casserole in the broiler 5-6 inches from heat. Broil for 1 minute or until the casserole is golden.

Nutritional Analysis

Calories	203	10 %	Total Fat	4.2 g.	6 %
Protein	13 g.	26 %	Cholesterol	9 mg.	5 %
Carbohydrate	31 g.	9 %	Sodium	411 mg.	12 %

Calories From Protein: 25% Carbohydrate: 58% Fat: 18%

Fancy Cut Baked Potatoes

SERVINGS: 4   PREPARATION TIME: 20 Minutes
SERVING SIZE: 1 Potato   COOKING TIME: 35 Minutes

4	Med.	Potatoes, raw, peeled
2	TBS.	Butter substitute, Butter Buds
2	TBS.	Chives
2	TBS.	Thyme, ground
2	TBS.	Parsley, dried
1/2 - 1 oz.		Cheddar cheese, low fat

1. Peel potatoes, removing all blemishes.

2. Cutting potato vertically, cut them into thin slices, but stop before you cut completely through. This type of cutting will give a fanned look . You can place a wooden spoon or object under knife to prevent cutting all the way through.

3. Place in a baking dish. Sprinkle with butter substitute and herbs.

4. Bake at 425 ° for approximately 45 minutes. Remove from oven and sprinkle cheese over top, and cook again for an additional 10 minutes.

*HINTS: Check baked potato at 45 minutes with a toothpick to see if done. Potato should be soft. Ovens may vary in temperature and may take longer to bake. Potatoes should be done before placing the cheese on top.

Nutritional Analysis

Calories	132	7 %	Total Fat	1.8 g.	2 %
Protein	5.8 g.	11 %	Cholesterol	5.3 mg.	3 %
Carbohydrate	25 g.	7 %	Sodium	298 mg.	9 %

Calories From Protein: 17 % Carbohydrate 72 % Fat: 12 %

Mashed Potatoes

SERVINGS: 2
SERVING SIZE: 1 1/2 Cups

3	Med.	Potato, raw without skin
1/4	C.	Butter substitute, Butter Buds
1/4	C.	Milk, skim
	Dash	Pepper
	Dash	Salt

1. Cut and quarter potatoes.

2. In a large sauce pan, place potatoes with enough water to cover them and boil. Cook until potatoes are soft when pierced with a fork.

3. Remove from heat, and drain off water.

4. Place in large bowl and add butter buds, salt and pepper. Mix with a mixer until smooth. Add a little of the milk as you go to make potatoes fluffier. Stop adding milk when desired texture is obtained.

Nutritional Analysis

Calories	173	9%	Total Fat	.21 g.	0%
Protein	4.5 g.	9%	Cholesterol	.5mg.	0%
Carbohydrate	44g.	12%	Sodium	591 mg.	18%

Calories from Protein: 9% Carbohydrate: 90% Fat: 1%

Mushroom Asparagus Omelet

SERVINGS: 2
SERVING SIZE: 1 Omelet

PREPARATION TIME: 15 Minutes
COOKING TIME: 25 Minutes

10	oz.	Asparagus, frozen 1 pkg.	3	tsp.	Butter substitute, liquid
1	C.	Mushrooms, sliced	1	TBS.	Soy sauce
1/4	C.	Onion, chopped	2	tsp.	Cornstarch
5	TBS.	Water	3/4	C.	Egg substitute

Preheat oven to 325 °.

1. Beat eggs until frothy, add 2 tablespoons water, and continue beating about 1 1/2 minutes or until stiff peaks form.

2. In a 10 inch skillet with an oven-proof handle, heat 1 tablespoon butter substitute until a drop of water sizzles.

3. Pour egg mixture, mounding it slightly higher at the sides.

4. Cook over low heat for about 8 - 10 minutes or until eggs are puffed, and set. Bottom may be a golden brown.

5. Place skillet in oven at 325 °. Bake for 10 minutes or until knife inserted in center comes out clean.

6. While waiting for eggs to cook, break asparagus apart, and if not yet thawed, run cold water over them.

7. In a small skillet, cook onion, 1 tablespoon butter substitute until tender, but not brown.

8. Add Asparagus and mushrooms. Cook and stir 3 - 4 minutes

9. Combine 4 tablespoons water, soy sauce, cornstarch, and stir into vegetable mixture.

10. Cook and stir until mixture is thick and bubbly. Continue to cook for about 1-2 more minutes

11. Remove eggs from oven, loosen sides of omelet with a spatula. On one side of eggs, fill center of omelet with vegetable mixture. Fold empty side over onto vegetable mixture (making like a sandwich). Slide off , onto plate and serve.

Nutritional Analysis

Calories	141	7 %	Total Fat	3.1 g.	4 %
Protein	14.6 g.	29 %	Cholesterol	107 mg.	53 %
Carbohydrate	13 5 g.	4 %	Sodium	654 mg.	20 %

Calories from Protein: 42 % Carbohydrate: 38 % Fat: 20 %

Potato Pancakes

SERVINGS: 2
SERVING SIZE: 3 Small

PREPARATION TIME: 25 Minutes
COOKING TIME: 10 Minutes

1 1/2	Med.	Potato, peeled, skinless
1	Lg.	Egg white
1/2	tsp.	Onion powder
2	TBS.	Oatmeal, dry
	Dash	Pepper
1	tsp.	Butter substitute, Butter Buds
	Dash	Salt, lite (optional)

1. Peel and grate potatoes. In a large bowl mix together all ingredients until well mixed together.

2. Preheat non stick fry pan over medium heat or use a pan coated with a non stick spray. Make 5 - 6 patties by hand and place them in the heated pan. Brown and turn over. Do not turn over more than once, as pancakes will break.

*TIP: If a mashed potato affect is wished, place all ingredients into a food processor, or blender, and mix until smooth.

Nutritional Analysis

Calories	104	5 %	Total Fat	.58 g.	1 %
Protein	4.8 g.	9 %	Cholesterol	0 mg.	0 %
Carbohydrate	21.2 g.	6 %	Sodium	128 mg.	4 %

Calories from Protein: 18 % Carbohydrate: 78 % Fat: 5 %

8

SWEETS AND SNACKS

Apple Crisp

PREPARATION TIME: 30 Minutes
COOKING TIME: 40 Minutes

5	C.	Apples, peeled and sliced
2	TBS.	Lemon juice
1/4	tsp.	Cinnamon
1/8	tsp.	Nutmeg
1/2	C.	Sugar, brown
1/2	C.	Oatmeal, dry
1/3	C.	Butter substitute, Butter Buds
		Non-stick cooking spray

Preheat oven to 375 °.

1. Spray a 2 quart casserole dish or cake pan (13" X 9" X 2") with non-stick cooking spray. Arrange apples in pan. Sprinkle with lemon and cinnamon.

2. In a medium bowl combine flour, brown sugar and oatmeal. Mix in butter substitute. Mixture should be crumbly and moist.

3. Spread over fruit and bake 40 minutes, or until apples are tender.

Nutritional Analysis

Calories	168	8 %	Total Fat	.99 g.	1 %
Protein	1.83 g.	4 %	Cholesterol	0 mg.	0 %
Carbohydrate	43 g.	12 %	Sodium	186 mg.	6 %

Calories from Protein: 4 %   Carbohydrate: 91 %   Fat: 5 %

Baked Custard

6	Lg.	Egg whites (or 3/4 cup egg substitute)
1/3	C.	Sugar
3	C.	Milk, skim, scalded
1/2	tsp.	Vanilla
1/4	tsp.	Nutmeg
1/4	tsp.	Salt (optional)

Preheat oven to 350 °.

1. Combine eggs, sugar, and salt (if using).

2. Add Milk slowly, stirring constantly.

3. Add vanilla, and mix in well.

4. Sprinkle in nutmeg.

5. Pour into custard cups, and place cups in a pan of hot water, bake 30 to 35 minutes at 350 °.

Nutritional Analysis

Calories	120	6 %	Total Fat	1.3 g.	2 %
Protein	10.2 g.	20 %	Cholesterol	2 mg.	1 %
Carbohydrate	16 g.	5 %	Sodium	203 mg.	6 %

Calories from Protein: 35 % Carbohydrate: 55 % Fat: 10 %

Christy's Carrot Cake

SERVINGS: 12
SERVING SIZE: 1 Piece

PREPARATION TIME: 45 Minutes
COOKING TIME: 45 - 60 Minutes

2	C.	Flour, whole wheat
1	C.	Sugar
10	pkt.	Sweet 'n Low
1	tsp.	Baking powder
1	tsp.	Baking soda
1	tsp.	Salt
1	tsp.	Cinnamon
3	C.	Carrots, diced
3	TBS.	Margarine, imitation, low fat
1/4	C.	Applesauce, canned, no sugar
4	Lg.	Egg whites

Preheat oven to 325 °.

Grease and lightly flour a large 13 x 9 x 2" or two 9" round layer cake pans.

1. In a large bowl combine all dry ingredients.

2. Add carrots, eggs and margarine.

3. Mix until moist.

4. Beat at medium speed for 2 minutes.

5. Bake at 325 ° for 45 - 60 minutes.

6. Let cool.

7. Frost with homemade cream cheese frosting in this section.

Nutritional Analysis

Calories	204	10 %	Total Fat	1.8 g.	2 %
Protein	4.1 g.	8 %	Cholesterol	0 mg.	0 %
Carbohydrate	44 g.	13 %	Sodium	352 mg.	11 %

Calories from Protein: 8 %   Carbohydrate: 84 %   Fat: 8 %

Chocolate Cake

SERVINGS: 16
SERVING SIZE: 1 - 2" Slice

PREPARATION TIME: 25 Minutes
COOKING TIME: 35 Minutes

1 1/4	C.	All purpose flour
1	C.	Sugar
1/2	C.	Cocoa, unsweetened powder
2	TBL.	Cornstarch
1	tsp.	Baking soda
4	Lg.	Egg whites
1	C.	Water
1/2	C.	Margarine, imitation, low fat
1/4	C.	Sugar, brown

Preheat oven to 350 °.

1. Spray an 8 or 9" baking pan with a low fat cooking spray.

2. In a large bowl, combine flour, sugars, cocoa, cornstarch, and baking soda.

3. In a medium bowl, whisk egg whites, water and margarine together.

4. Add to flour mixture. Mix until batter is smooth.

5. Pour into pan and bake at 350 ° for approximately 35 minutes, or until an inserted toothpick in the center of the cake comes out clean.

Nutritional Analysis

Calories	134	7 %	Total Fat	3.14 g.	4 %
Protein	2.26 g.	4 %	Cholesterol	1 mg.	1 %
Carbohydrate	24.7 g.	7 %	Sodium	141 mg.	4 %

Calories From Protein: 7% Carbohydrate: 73% Fat: 21%

Chocolate Chip Brownies

SERVINGS: 36
SERVING SIZE: 1 - 2" Square

PREPARATION TIME: 20 Minutes
COOKING TIME: 25 Minutes

1	C.	Flour, all purpose
1 3/4	C.	Sugar, or sugar substitute
1	C.	Brown Sugar
6	Lg.	Egg whites, (or 3/4 cup egg substitute)
1/4	C.	Margarine, imitation, low fat or
		Prunes, baby
1/4	C.	Cocoa, unsweetened powder
1 1/2	tsp.	Vanilla
4	oz.	Chocolate chips, semi-sweet or sugar free
		chocolate bits

Preheat oven to 350 °.

1. In a large bowl, combine sugars, flour, egg whites, and margarine (or prunes) and cocoa. Mix well until blended. Stir in vanilla.

2. Add chocolate chips. Mix in well.

3. Spread into a nonfat greased 13 x 9 x 2" pan and bake for 25 minutes, or until done.

4. Cool in pan. (If a wire rack is available, place on rack, this is best way to cool).

Nutritional Analysis

Calories	98	5 %	Total Fat	1.82 g.	2 %
Protein	1.15 g.	2 %	Cholesterol	0.22 mg.	0 %
Carbohydrate	20 g.	6 %	Sodium	28 mg.	1 %

Calories from Protein: 5 %   Carbohydrate: 79 % Fat: 16%

Chocolate Chip Cookies

SERVINGS: 36
SERVING SIZE: 1 Cookie

PREPARATION TIME: 20 Minutes
COOKING TIME: 10 Minutes

1/2	C.	Sugar, or sugar substitute
2/3	C.	Butter substitute, liquid
2	Lg.	Egg whites
1	tsp.	Vanilla
2	C.	Flour, all purpose
1/2	tsp.	Baking Soda
6	oz.	Chocolate chips, semi-sweet, or sugar free chocolate bits.

Preheat oven to 375°.

1. Add butter substitute, sugar, egg whites, and vanilla together, and mix.

2. Stir together all dry ingredients in a separate bowl.

3. Add dry ingredients to butter mixture. Mix well with a wooden spoon.

4. Drop with a teaspoon onto a cookie sheet, placing about 1-1 1/2" apart.

5. Bake 8-10 minutes. After baking cookies will be slightly pale in color.

Nutritional Analysis

Calories	67	3%	Total Fat	1.06 g.	1%
Protein	09.7 g.	2%	Cholesterol	0mg.	0%
Carbohydrate	12.4g.	4%	Sodium	18.6 mg.	1%

Calories from Protein: 6% Carbohydrate: 79% Fat: 15%

Choc-Yogurt Creme Pudding

SERVINGS: 4   PREPARATION TIME: 10 Minutes
SERVING SIZE: 1/2 Cup   COOKING TIME: 15 Minutes

1/3	C.	Cocoa, unsweetened powder
1	pkt.	Gelatin, unflavored
1 1/3	C.	Milk, skim
16	fl. oz.	Yogurt, vanilla (1 container)
1	tsp.	Vanilla
1/4	C.	Strawberries
1/2	C.	Sugar

1. In a sauce pan stir together milk, sugar, cocoa and gelatin.

2. Add gelatin and bring to a boil and until gelatin is dissolved. Stir constantly.

3. Remove from heat, and cool about 5 minutes.

4. Add vanilla and yogurt.

5. Fold together, until well mixed. Pour into pudding or dessert dishes, and refrigerate until set. About 2-3 hours.

Nutritional Analysis

Calories	348	17 %	Total Fat	2.3 g.	3 %
Protein	11 g.	22 %	Cholesterol	9.2 mg.	5 %
Carbohydrate	72 g.	21 %	Sodium	136 mg.	4 %

Calories from Protein: 12 % Carbohydrate: 82 % Fat: 6 %

Coffee Cake

SERVINGS: 8
SERVING SIZE: 1 - 2" Slice

PREPARATION TIME: 30 Minutes
COOKING TIME: 30 Minutes

1 C. + 2 TBS.		Flour, all purpose
2 1/4	tsp.	Baking powder
1/3	C.	Sugar
1/2	C.	Applesauce, canned, no sugar
1/2	C.	Milk, skim
2	Lg.	Egg whites
1/2	C.	Sugar, brown
2	tsp.	Cinnamon
3/4	C.	Raisins

TOPPING:

1/2	C.	Flour, all purpose
1/4	C.	Applesauce, canned, no sugar
1		Egg white
1/2	C.	Brown Sugar
3/4	C.	Raisins

Preheat oven to 375 °.

1. Sift together 1/2 cup flour, baking powder, and granulated sugar. Set aside.

2. Blend 1/2 the milk and 2 egg whites with a fork; add to dry ingredients.

3. Stir applesauce with a wooden spoon until flour mixture is moistened. Set aside.

4. Making layers, spread half of the batter in an 8" round Teflon cake pan; sprinkle with half of the topping. Add the remaining batter; sprinkle with remaining topping. Bake at 375 ° for 30 minutes.

Nutritional Analysis

Calories	202	10 %	Total Fat	0.28 g.	0 %
Protein	3.6 g.	7 %	Cholesterol	0.25 mg.	0 %
Carbohydrate	48 g.	14 %	Sodium	149 mg.	5 %

Calories From Protein: 7% Carbohydrate: 92% Fat: 1%

Cream Cheese Frosting

SERVINGS: 12
SERVING SIZE: Approximately 3 Tablespoons

PREPARATION TIME: 20 Minutes
COOKING TIME: 0

3	C.	Sugar, confectioner's
4	TBS.	Butter substitute, Butter Buds
1 1/2	tsp.	Vanilla extract
2	tsp.	Milk, skim
1	oz.	Cream cheese, light

1. Blend all ingredients together until smooth.

2. Refrigerate for Approx. 30 minutes before using.

*HINT: If the frosting is too creamy, add a tsp. of sugar at a time while mixing; if it is too stiff, add a tsp.   of milk at a time during mixing until desired texture.

*NOTE: Using a butter substitute may make frosting have a slight yellow tint. True frosting uses lard making frostings white.

Nutritional Analysis

Calories	1503	75	Total Fat	7 g.	9 %
Protein	3.35 g.	7	Cholesterol	25 mg.	13 %
Carbohydrate	372 g.	106	Sodium	1039 mg.	31 %

Calories from Protein: 1 % Carbohydrate: 95 % Fat: 4 %

Creamy Cheesecake

SERVINGS: 10
SERVING SIZE: 1 Slice

PREPARATION TIME: 25 Minutes
COOKING TIME: 50 Minutes

20		Crackers, graham w/sugar, honey
1/4	C.	Sugar, or sugar substitute
1/3	C.	Butter substitute, Liquid
16	oz.	Cream cheese, light or fat free
14	oz.	Milk, condensed, sweetened
6	Lg.	Egg whites
1/4	C.	Lemon juice, from concentrate
8	oz.	Yogurt, plain, nonfat

Preheat oven to 300 °.

1. Crush graham crackers to semi-fine crumbs.

2. Combine crumbs, sugar, and butter substitute. Mix until crumbly. Press firmly on bottom of a 9" springform pan.

3. In a large mixer bowl, beat cheese until fluffy.

4. Gradually beat sweetened condensed milk in until smooth.

5. Add eggs and lemon juice. Mix well.

6. Pour into prepared pan. Bake for 50 minutes or until center is set.

7. Cool and chill. Can be served with a fruit topping for added flavor.

*HINT: Using a fat free cream cheese will lower the fat percentage of each slice.

Nutritional Analysis

Calories	461	23 %	Total Fat	18.7 g.	25 %
Protein	13.5 g.	26 %	Cholesterol	57 mg.	28 %
Carbohydrate	58 g.	17 %	Sodium	433 mg.	13 %

Calories from Protein: 12 % Carbohydrate: 51 % Fat: 37 %

Dana's Lemon Poppy Seed Cake

SERVINGS: 24
SERVING SIZE: 1 Slice

PREPARATION TIME: 1 Hour
COOKING TIME: 40 Minutes

1	Box	Cake mix, yellow, lite or fat free
1/2	C.	Sugar
1/3	C.	Applesauce, canned/sweet
1/4	C.	Water
1	C.	Yogurt, plain, nonfat
8	Lg.	Egg white, (or 1 cup egg substitute)
3	TBS.	Lemon juice
2	TBS.	Poppy seeds

GLAZE:

1/2	C.	Sugar, powdered
2	TBS.	Lemon juice

Preheat oven to 350 °.

1. Combine cake mix and sugar in a large mixing bowl.

2. Add applesauce, water, yogurt, egg whites, and lemon juice. Beat at medium speed with an electric mixer. Approximately 6 minutes.

3. Stir in poppy seeds.

4. Pour batter into a 10 cup bundt pan coated with cooking spray.

5. Bake at 350 ° for 40 minutes, or until a toothpick inserted in center of cake comes out clean.

6. Cool on pan or a wire rack for 10 minutes. Remove from pan.

7. Mix glaze mixture, and when cake is completely cooled, drizzle over top of cake.

Nutritional Analysis

Calories	132	7 %	Total Fat	1.84 g.	2 %
Protein	2.27 g.	4 %	Cholesterol	0 mg.	0 %
Carbohydrate	26 g.	7 %	Sodium	181 mg.	5 %

Calories from Protein: 7 %   Carbohydrate: 80 % Fat: 13 %

Fruit Flan

PREPARATION TIME: 45 Minutes
COOKING TIME: 30 Minutes

3	C.	Strawberries
2	cans, 16 oz.	Peaches, condensed, light syrup
2	Med.	Kiwis
3	C.	Custard or Vanilla pudding mix, low calorie
1/2	C.	Corn syrup
1/4	C.	Sugar

1. Use a pastry shell for the crust. Recipe is in this section.

2. Mix custard pudding to directions on the package (using skim milk rather than specified).

3. Wash and slice strawberries into halves lengthwise. Set aside.

4. Drain juice from peaches, and set aside.

5. Peel and cut kiwi slices into thin slices width wise.

6. When pie shell has been baked and cooled, place pudding in shell. Smooth with spatula.

7. Line strawberries around outer edge of pie with pointed ends up.

8. Overlap peaches slightly onto strawberries and line the next section with peaches in a circle, with rounded edges up.

9. Next fill the center with kiwi's, overlapping until the center hole is filled.

GLAZE: In a small sauce pan, over medium heat, heat corn syrup and sugar until sugar is dissolved. Cool slightly, and pour a thin coat over the top of fruit. This will give the pie a shinny effect.

Nutritional Analysis

Calories	226	11 %	Total Fat	0.49 g.	1 %
Protein	4.34 g.	9 %	Cholesterol	1.5 mg.	1 %
Carbohydrate	54 g.	15 %	Sodium	121 mg.	4 %

Calories From Protein: 7% Carbohydrate: 91% Fat: 2%

Fruit in a Cloud Pie

SERVINGS: 10
SERVING SIZE: 1 Slice

PREPARATION TIME: 30 Minutes
COOKING TIME: 1-1/2 Hours

6	Lg.	Egg whites, (or equivalent egg substitute)
1/4	tsp.	Cream of Tartar
1 1/2	tsp.	Vanilla
1/2	lb.	Blueberries
2	Med.	Banana's
1	lb.	Strawberries
1	TBS.	Lemon juice

Heat oven to 225 °.

1. Slice fruit, mix all together except banana's. Set aside in refrigerator.

2. Beat egg whites until foamy.

3. Add cream of tartar. Beat to firm peaks. Gradually add vanilla. Mash banana's, add to mixture and continue mixing.

4. Spread mixture evenly in a 9" pie plate.

5. Bake crust for 1 1/2 hours. Turn oven off and cool baked shell inside oven, about 30-40 minutes

6. Place fruit mixture in shell and serve.

Nutritional Analysis

Calories	61	3 %	Total Fat	0.42 g.	1 %
Protein	2.47 g.	5 %	Cholesterol	0 mg.	0 %
Carbohydrate	13 g.	4 %	Sodium	33.5 mg.	1 %

Calories from Protein: 15 % Carbohydrate: 79 % Fat: 6 %

Homemade Applesauce

SERVINGS: 2
SERVING SIZE: 1/2 Cup

PREPARATION TIME: 15 Minutes
COOKING TIME: 25 Minutes

5	Med.	Apples
1	C.	Apple juice
1/4	tsp.	Cinnamon
1/4	tsp.	Nutmeg

1. Peel and core apples, then cut into quarters. Place in cold water, with a little salt (to prevent browning until apples are cut and used).

2. Place apples in a large sauce pan with enough water to cover bottom of pan, to prevent apples from burning. Cook over medium heat until apples are soft and mushy. Add cinnamon and nutmeg.

3. Remove from heat and cool.

*HINT: If cooked apples are in undesirable sized chunks, place in food processor, and blend adding enough apple juice to make a thick soupy texture.

Nutritional analysis

Calories	263	13 %	Total Fat	1.5 g.	2 %
Protein	0.87 g.	2 %	Cholesterol	0 mg.	0 %
Carbohydrate	67 g.	19 %	Sodium	6.1 mg.	0 %

Calories From Protein: 1 % Carbohydrate: 94% Fat: 5%

Impossible Pumpkin Pie

SERVINGS: 10
SERVING SIZE: 1 Slice

PREPARATION TIME: 15 Minutes
COOKING TIME: 55 Minutes

3/4	C.	Sugar
1/2	C.	Pancake mix or Bisquick
2	TBS.	Butter substitute, dry
13	fl oz.	Milk, evaporated, skim
4	Lg.	Egg whites (or 1/2 cup egg substitute)
2 1/2	C.	Pumpkin, canned (16 oz. can)
2 1/2	tsp.	Pumpkin pie spice
2	tsp.	Vanilla

Preheat oven to 350 °.

1. Put all ingredients in a blender, and blend until smooth.

2. Pour into a non fat greased pie plate (9 x 1 1/4" or 10 x 1 1/2")

3. Bake at 350 ° for 50 - 55 minutes or until knife in center comes out clean.

Nutritional Analysis

Calories	149	7 %	Total Fat	1.03 g.	1 %
Protein	5.4 g.	11 %	Cholesterol	1.3 mg.	1 %
Carbohydrate	28 g.	8 %	Sodium	146 mg.	4 %

Calories from Protein: 15 % Carbohydrate: 79 % Fat: 6 %

Irresistible Cookies

SERVINGS: 16
SERVING SIZE: 2 Cookies

PREPARATION TIME: 20 Minutes
COOKING TIME: 15 Minutes

1	C.	Butter substitute, liquid (or applesauce)
1	C.	Sugar (or equivalent sugar substitute)
2	Lg. +	Egg whites
1	Lg.	Egg (or 3/4 C. egg substitute)
1	tsp.	Vanilla
2	C.	Flour
1/2	tsp.	Baking powder
1	tsp.	Baking soda
2	C.	Oats, rolled, quick
2	C.	Corn flakes, (or equivalent, to Wheaties)

Preheat oven to 350 °.

1. Mix Butter substitute, sugar, egg whites, egg (or egg substitute), and vanilla together.

2. In another bowl mix flour, baking powder, baking soda, oats, and corn flakes together.

3. Add dry ingredients to wet, and mix thoroughly.

4. Drop onto a cookie sheet by a fork (If fork is wet, it may work better). Spread with fork, leaving about 1" between cookies. Bake for 15 minutes at 350 °.

Nutritional Analysis

Calories	175	9 %	Total Fat	1.24 g.	2 %
Protein	4.2 g.	8 %	Cholesterol	13.3 mg.	7 %
Carbohydrate	32 g.	9 %	Sodium	104 mg.	3 %

Calories from Protein: 11 % Carbohydrates: 82 % Fat: 7 %

Kiwi And Snow Jelly

SERVINGS: 4
SERVING SIZE: 1 - 2" Slice

PREPARATION TIME: 1 Hour and 30 Minutes
REFRIGERATION TIME: 1 Hour

3	Med.	Kiwi
1/2	TBS.	Agar powder
1/4	C.	Sugar
2	C.	Water
2	Lg.	Egg white
1	TBS.	Lemon juice

1. Mix agar powder and 2 cups water in a sauce pan. Heat to a full boil. Stir well until agar is dissolved.

2. Lower heat to medium low and add sugar. Cook until sugar is dissolved.

3. With an electric mixer, beat egg whites until soft peaks form.

4. Slowly add agar liquid to egg whites while still mixing.

5. Continue beating until liquid is finely combined. Add lemon juice. Continue beating for approximately 1 minute more.

6. Rinse a jelly mold or round plastic container with water. This will prevent the fruit from sticking to pan.

7. Arrange kiwi's first on bottom of mold or container. Spread egg white mixture over kiwi's and refrigerate for approximately 1 hour.

*HINT: Six sliced strawberries can be used in replace of kiwi's.

Nutritional Analysis

Calories	303	15 %	Total Fat	0.25 g.	0 %
Protein	2.75 g.	5 %	Cholesterol	0 mg.	0 %
Carbohydrate	74 g.	21 %	Sodium	42 mg.	1 %

Calories From Protein: 4% Carbohydrate: 96% Fat: 1%

Marshmallow Frosting

SERVINGS: 24
SERVING SIZE: 4 Tablespoons

PREPARATION TIME: 20 Minutes
COOKING TIME: 0

4	Lg.	Egg whites
1 1/2	C.	Sugar
1/2	tsp.	Cream of tartar
1/3	C.	Water
1	tsp.	Vanilla extract

1. Mix powdered sugar and cream of tartar together and set aside.

2. Beat egg whites until stiff peaks form. Slowly add in vanilla.

3. When stiff peaks are formed slowly add powdered sugar mixture to egg whites. Frosting will cover one, 2-layered, 8" round cake.

Nutritional Analysis

Calories	51	3 %	Total Fat	0 g.	0 %
Protein	0.58 g.	1 %	Cholesterol	0 mg.	0 %
Carbohydrate	12 g.	3 %	Sodium	11.2 mg.	0 %

Calories From Protein: 5% Carbohydrate: 95% Fat: 0%

No Bake Cheese Cake

SERVINGS: 12
SERVING SIZE: 1 Slice

PREPARATION TIME: 30 Minutes
REFRIGERATION TIME: 2 Hours

20		Crackers, graham w/sugar, honey
1/2	C.	Butter substitute, liquid
1/2	C.	Sugar, brown, low calorie
1	C.	Jell-O, lemon
8	oz.	Cream cheese, light or fat free
1	C.	Sugar, or a sugar substitute
1	tsp.	Vanilla
1/2	C.	Milk evaporated, whole milk (DO NOT use evaporated SKIM)

1. Crush graham crackers into fine crumbs. Set about 3 Tablespoons aside.

2. Mix together graham crackers, butter substitute, and brown sugar until crumbly.

3. Spread crust mixture over the bottom of a 13 x 9 x 2" pan. Pat down firm.

4. Dissolve jello in 1 cup hot water, and let cool.

5. Cream together 8 oz. of cream cheese and sugar. Add vanilla, and jello mix. Mix well.

6. Whip evaporated milk until stiff peaks form. If the bowl, beaters, and milk are refrigerated ahead of time, whipping will go much faster.

7. Fold in other ingredients to whipped milk.

8. Pour mixture over cracker crumb crust. Sprinkle the 3 Tablespoons over the top for added decoration.

   *HINT: Using a fat free cream cheese will lower the fat percentage in the Nutritional Analysis.

Nutritional Analysis

Calories	270	14 %	Total Fat	7.8 g.	10 %
Protein	4.2 g.	8 %	Cholesterol	18.2 mg.	9 %
Carbohydrate	44 g.	13 %	Sodium	212 mg.	6 %

Calories from Protein: 6 % Carbohydrates: 67 % Fat: 27 %

Pastry Pie Shell

SERVINGS: 8
SERVING SIZE: 1/8 Pie, 1 Slice

PREPARATION TIME: 35-40 Minutes
COOKING TIME: 0

2	C.	All purpose flour
8	TBS.	Margarine, imitation, low fat
4-6	TBS.	Water

Makes 1-8" 2 layered pie shell.

Preheat oven to 475°.

1. Mix all ingredients together with a fork. Mix until thoroughly moist, but do not over work.

2. Shape into two separate balls. On a floured cutting board, roll out pastry until a large enough circle is formed to cover the bottom of the pie pan.

3. Careful not to tear the crust, fold in half, and then in half again (making a triangle). Pick up the crust, and place in the pie pan and unfold.

4. With a knife, cut off the excess dough around the edges of the pan.

5. Add excess to next ball of dough, roll out and do same for top crust. If a top crust is not needed for your recipe, dough may be wrapped in plastic wrap and frozen to save for future use. Saves about 2 weeks in freezer.

Nutritional Analysis

Calories	155	8%	Total Fat	6.3 g.	8%
Protein	3 g.	6%	Cholesterol	0mg.	0%
Carbohydrate	22.4g.	6%	Sodium	111 mg.	3%

Calories from Protein: 8% Carbohydrate: 56% Fat: 36%

198

Quick Cocoa Cupcakes

PREPARATION TIME: 10 Minutes
COOKING TIME: 20 Minutes

1/2	C.	Prunes, baby (or butter substitute)
1	C.	Sugar
2	Lg.	Egg whites
1 1/3	C.	Flour, all purpose
1	tsp.	Baking powder
1/2	tsp.	Baking soda
1/2	C.	Cocoa
1/2	C.	Milk, skim
1	tsp.	Vanilla
1/2	C.	Coffee, hot

Preheat oven to 375 °.

1. In a large bowl mix prunes, sugar, and egg whites together, beat well.

2. In another bowl, add flour, baking powder, soda, and cocoa. Mix well.

3. Add dry ingredients to wet, then add in milk and vanilla. Mix well.

4. Next add coffee. Mix well.

5. Grease cupcake tins with a non stick spray or use paper liners. Fill cupcake pans about 2/3 from the top.

6. Bake for 20 minutes at 375 °.

*NOTE: Powdered sugar may be sprinkled over top for frosting, or a chocolate or vanilla frosting may be used.

Nutritional Analysis

Calories	92	5 %	Total Fat	0.20 g.	0 %
Protein	1.9 g.	4 %	Cholesterol	1 mg.	1 %
Carbohydrate	18.7 g.	5 %	Sodium	74 mg.	2 %

Calories from Fat: 9 % Carbohydrate: 89 % Fat: 2 %

Rice Pudding

1/2	C.	Rice, uncooked
3	C.	Milk, skim
2/3	C.	Sugar
3	Lg.	Egg whites, or substitute
1	tsp.	Vanilla
1	C.	Raisins, (optional)
	Dash	Nutmeg

Preheat oven to 350 °.

1. Cook rice in steamer until tender, about 25 minutes. (1/2 cup rice to 1/2 cup water exactly).

2. Beat egg whites (or substitutes) and add sugar. Mix well.

3. Add milk to eggs and sugar.

4. Add cooked rice, raisins, and vanilla.

5. Pour into baking dish (or casserole pan), place baking dish inside a pan of hot water. Bake for approximately 45 minutes, or until a metal knife inserted to center comes out clean.

Nutritional Analysis

Calories	201	10 %	Total Fat	1.16 g.	2 %
Protein	8 g.	16 %	Cholesterol	1.5 mg.	1 %
Carbohydrate	41 g.	12 %	Sodium	93 mg.	3 %

Calories from Protein: 16 % Carbohydrate: 79 % Fat: 5 %

Sea Foam Frosting

SERVINGS: 1
SERVING SIZE: 8 " Round Cake (2 Layer)

PREPARATION TIME: 10 Minutes
COOKING TIME: 15 Minutes

2	Lg.	Egg whites
3/4	C.	Brown sugar
1/3	C.	Corn Syrup
2	TBS.	Water
1/4	tsp.	Cream of tartar
1	TBS.	Vanilla
2	TBS.	Semi-sweet chips (or sugar free chocolate chips)

1. Cook egg whites, brown sugar, corn syrup, water, and cream of tartar, over boiling water in a double boiler, beating with an electric mixer until mixture stands in peaks.

2. Remove from heat and add 1 tablespoon vanilla, and continue beating until thick enough to spread.

3. Gently fold in 2 tablespoons of semi-sweet chocolate morsels. DO NOT STIR.

4. Frost cooled layers of cake.

Nutritional Analysis

Calories	1103	55 %	Total Fat	5.8 g.	8 %
Protein	8.2 g.	16 %	Cholesterol	0 mg.	0 %
Carbohydrate	258 g.	74 %	Sodium	270 mg.	8 %

Calories from Protein: 3 %   Carbohydrate: 92 % Fat: 5 %

Sour Cream Cookies

SERVINGS: 16
SERVING SIZE: 2 Cookies

PREPARATION TIME: 15 Minutes
COOKING TIME: 12 -15 Minutes

1	C.	Sugar (or equivalent substitute)
1	C.	Sour cream, low fat
2	Lg.	Egg whites
2	C.	Flour
1/2	tsp.	Baking soda
1	tsp.	Vanilla
1/4	tsp.	Nutmeg

Preheat oven to 400 °.

1. In a large bowl, mix all ingredients together until well mixed.

2. Drop onto cookie sheet with a spoon about 1 inch apart.

3. Bake in 400 ° oven, for approximately 12 to 15 minutes. Makes 32 cookies.

Nutritional Analysis

Calories	112	6 %	Total Fat	0.37 g.	0 %
Protein	2.7 g.	5 %	Cholesterol	0.88 mg.	0 %
Carbohydrate	24 g.	7 %	Sodium	43.4 mg.	1 %

Calories from Protein: 10 % Carbohydrate: 87 % Fat: 3 %

Spicy Applesauce Cookies

SERVINGS: 5
SERVING SIZE: 2 Cookies

PREPARATION TIME: 20 Minutes
COOKING TIME: 12 Minutes

2	C.	Flour, all purpose
1 1/2	C.	Sugar, brown
1/2	C.	Butter substitute, liquid, Butter Buds
2	Lg.	Egg whites
1	tsp.	Vanilla extract
3/4	C.	Applesauce, canned, no sugar
1/2	tsp.	Pumpkin pie spice
1	tsp.	Baking powder
1	tsp.	baking soda

Preheat oven to 375 °.

1. Cream together sugar and butter buds.

2. Beat in egg whites and vanilla.

3. Stir in applesauce.

4. Combine flour, spice, baking powder and soda.

5. Stir into creamed mixture.

6. Drop by teaspoonfuls onto low fat greased cookie sheet. Bake at 375 ° for about 12 minutes. Cool on racks.

Nutritional Analysis

Calories	473	24 %	Total Fat	0.77 g.	1 %
Protein	6.3 g.	12 %	Cholesterol	0 mg.	0 %
Carbohydrate	104 g.	30 %	Sodium	295 mg.	9 %

Calories From Protein: 6% Carbohydrate: 93% Fat: 2%

9

BEVERAGES

Chocolate Milkshake

SERVINGS: 2
SERVING SIZE: 1 1/2 Cup

PREPARATION TIME: 15 Minutes
COOKING TIME: 0

1	C.	Frozen Yogurt, vanilla
1	C.	Milk, skim
1	pkt.	Cocoa mix, dry
1	C.	Ice

1. Place all items in blender, and put setting on frappe.

2. Blend until milk shake consistency occurs.

*NOTE: If not thick enough, add more ice. If too thin, add more yogurt.
Adding more yogurt will change the nutritional analysis.

Nutritional Analysis

Calories	218	11 %	Total Fat	4.6 g.	6 %
Protein	7.8 g.	15 %	Cholesterol	9 mg.	5 %
Carbohydrate	35 g.	10 %	Sodium	200 mg.	6 %

Calories From Protein: 15 % Carbohydrate: 66 % Fat: 19 %

Cranberry Pineapple punch

SERVINGS: 3
SERVING SIZE: 1 Cup

PREPARATION TIME: 15 Minutes
COOKING TIME: 0

1/2	C.	Pineapple, canned in juice
1 1/4	C.	Cranberry juice cocktail, low calorie
2	TBS.	Lemon juice
1	C.	Water, carbonated

1. Place pineapple chunks in blender. Blend until pulp.

2. Add cranberry juice, lemon juice and carbonated water to blender with pineapple. Blend.

3. Serve with ice.

*HINT: If a sweeter flavor is desired, substitute 7-Up for water.

Nutritional Analysis

Calories	47	2 %	Total Fat	0.06 g.	0 %
Protein	0.21 g.	0 %	Cholesterol	0 mg.	0 %
Carbohydrate	12.2 g.	3 %	Sodium	9.3 mg.	0 %

Calories from Protein: 2 %   Carbohydrate: 97 % Fat: 1%

Fabulous Fruity Punch

SERVINGS: 8
SERVING SIZE: 1 Cup

PREPARATION TIME: 20 Minutes
COOKING TIME: 0

3	C.	Water
4	tsp.	Sugar, (or equivalent sugar substitute)
2	Med.	Banana
24	fl. oz.	Pineapple juice
6	fl. oz.	Orange juice, frozen concentrate
6	fl. oz.	Lemonade, concentrate
28	fl. oz.	Water, carbonated.

1. Add water, with sugar (or sugar substitute). Mix slowly until dissolved. Set aside.

2. Combine in a blender, Banana's, half of the pineapple juice. Blend thoroughly.

3. Stir banana mixture into water and sugar. Add pineapple juice, orange juice, and lemonade concentrate.

4. Add carbonated water to mixture slowly. Freezing mixture until needed is possible. Take from freezer 30 minutes before use. Add ice if desired, and garnish with fruit.

Nutritional Analysis

Calories	108	5 %	Total Fat	0.24 g.	0 %
Protein	0.77 g.	2 %	Cholesterol	0 mg.	0 %
Carbohydrate	27 g.	8 %	Sodium	7.5 mg.	0 %

Calories from Protein: 3 % Carbohydrate: 95 % Fat: 2 %

Hot Apple Cider

SERVINGS: 8
SERVING SIZE: 8 Fluid Ounces

PREPARATION TIME: 10 Minutes
COOKING TIME: 20 Minutes

3	C.	Apple cider juice
1/2	C.	Sugar, brown, low calorie
	Dash	Nutmeg
1/2	tsp.	Cinnamon
1	tsp.	Allspice
1	tsp.	Cloves, ground

1. In a large saucepan combine all ingredients. Bring to boil.

2. Reduce heat; cover and simmer 10 minutes.

3. Serve cider in mugs.

*HINT: Can be served with a slice of orange.

Nutritional Analysis

Calories	156	8 %	Total Fat	0.37 g.	0 %
Protein	0.18 g.	0 %	Cholesterol	0 mg.	0 %
Carbohydrate	40.5 g.	12 %	Sodium	11.9 mg.	0 %

Calories From Protein: 0% Carbohydrate: 98% Fat: 2%

Hot Chocolate

SERVINGS:: 7
SERVING SIZE: 1 Cup

PREPARATION TIME: 15 Minutes
COOKING TIME: 15 Minutes

1/2	C.	Water
1/2	TBS.	Sugar
1	tsp.	Nutmeg
5	C.	Milk, skim
1/2	C.	Whipped topping, Dream Whip or low fat Whipped cream
3	oz.	Chocolate morsels, semi-sweet, Chocolate Chips

To prepare:

1. In large saucepan, combine chocolate morsels and water over low heat, stirring constantly.

2. Blend in sugar and salt; simmer 4 minutes, stirring occasionally.

3. Fold in Cream. Refrigerate until service time.

To serve:

1. Heat milk to scalding.

2. Place 1 heaping tablespoon chocolate mixture in each cup; fill with hot milk. Mix well until chocolate is dissolved.

3. Sprinkle with nutmeg.

*NOTE: Chocolate mixture will keep up to 1 week in the refrigerator.

Nutritional Analysis

Calories	137	7 %	Total Fat	4.06 g.	5 %
Protein	6.6 g.	13 %	Cholesterol	2.86 mg.	1 %
Carbohydrate	19.6 g.	6 %	Sodium	98 mg.	3 %

Calories From Protein: 19% Carbohydrate: 55% Fat: 26%

211

Imitation Margarita

SERVINGS: 2
SERVING SIZE: 1 Cup

PREPARATION TIME: 15 Minutes
COOKING TIME: 0

1	TBS.	Lemon juice
1	TBS.	Lime Juice
1 1/2	C.	Lemonade or Margarita Mix, frozen concentrate
2	C.	Ice
1	Slice	Lime

1. Add all ingredients except lime slice to blender and frappe until desired consistency is acquired.

2. If too thick add a little lemonade at a time and blend.

Nutritional Analysis

Calories	78	4 %	Total Fat	0.11 g.	0 %
Protein	0.17 g.	0 %	Cholesterol	0 mg.	0 %
Carbohydrate	21 g.	6 %	Sodium	14 mg.	0 %

Calories From Protein: 1% Carbohydrate: 98% Fat: 1%

Imitation Strawberry Daiquiri

SERVINGS: 2
SERVING SIZE: 1 Cup

PREPARATION TIME: 20 Minutes
COOKING TIME: 0

1	C.	Lemonade, frozen concentrate or Sweet and Sour liquor mix
1/2	C.	Strawberries
2	TBS.	Sugar
2	C.	Ice

1. Add strawberries and sugar to blender and puree.

2. Add lemonade and ice. Frappe to desired consistency.

*HINT: If garnish is desired: Leave one strawberry whole. Cut a slice lengthwise in strawberry and slide onto edge of glass.

Nutritional Analysis

Calories	157	8 %	Total Fat	0.25 g.	0 %
Protein	0.33 g.	1 %	Cholesterol	0 mg.	0 %
Carbohydrate	41 g.	12 %	Sodium	14.7 mg.	0 %

Calories From Protein: 1% Carbohydrate: 98% Fat: 1%

Strawberry Milkshake

SERVINGS: 2
SERVING SIZE: 1 Cup

PREPARATION TIME: 15 Minutes
COOKING TIME: 0

3/4	C.	Strawberries
1/2	C.	Frozen Yogurt, vanilla
1/2	C.	Milk, skim
2	TBS.	Sugar
1	C.	Ice

1. Place strawberries into blender with sugar and puree.

2. Add frozen yogurt, milk and ice. Frappe until milkshake consistency is acquired.

* NOTE: Top with fat free whipped cream. Or garnish with a whole strawberry on the side of the glass. Cut a slit in strawberry lengthwise and place on side of glass.

Nutritional Analysis

Calories	146	7%	Total Fat	2.3 g.	3%
Protein	3.74 g.	7%	Cholesterol	4.5mg.	2%
Carbohydrate	27.6g.	8%	Sodium	68 mg.	2%

Calories from Protein: 10% Carbohydrate: 76% Fat: 14%

10

SAUCES, DIPS & MISCELLANEOUS

Barbecue Sauce

SERVINGS: 4
SERVING SIZE: 1 Tablespoon

1/2	C	Ketchup, low sodium
1	TBS.	Water
1	TBS.	Honey
1	1/2 tsp.	Worcestershire sauce
1	tsp.	Mustard, yellow

Mix all ingredients together thoroughly in medium size bowl. Refrigerate until needed.

Nutritional Analysis

Calories	27.5	1 %	Total Fat	0.25 g.	0 %
Protein	0.69 g.	1 %	Cholesterol	0 mg.	0 %
Carbohydrate	6.7 g.	2 %	Sodium	255 mg.	8 %

Calories From Protein: 9% Carbohydrate: 84% Fat: 7%

Bean Dip

PREPARATION TIME: 20 Minutes
COOKING TIME: 0

15	oz.	Kidney beans, canned
3	TBS.	Water
1	TBS.	Vinegar
1	tsp.	Chili powder
1/8	tsp.	Cumin powder
2	tsp.	Parsley, fresh
2	tsp.	Onion, chopped

1. Drain kidney beans and rinse. (if using dried kidney beans, cook and rinse).

2. Place drained beans, vinegar, water and seasonings in a blender. Blend until smooth.

3. Remove from blender, and into a bowl, add onions and parsley.

4. Chill and serve with crisp vegetables, or on top of a taco salad.

- HINT: Removing juice from beans, and rinsing, will help stop the gassy effect of kidney beans.

Nutritional Analysis

Calories	92	5%	Total Fat	0.53 g.	1%
Protein	5.8 g.	11%	Cholesterol	0mg.	0%
Carbohydrate	17.6g.	5%	Sodium	377 mg.	11%

Calories from Protein: 24% Carbohydrate: 71% Fat: 5%

Dill and Mustard Dip

SERVINGS: 8
SERVING SIZE: 1 Tablespoon

PREPARATION TIME: 15 Minutes
COOKING TIME: 0

1/2	C.	Mayonnaise, nonfat
1	tsp.	Mustard, yellow
1/4	tsp.	Dill weed

In small bowl, combine all ingredients; mix well. Cover; refrigerate to chill.

Nutritional Analysis

Calories	10.6	1 %	Total Fat	0.02 g.	0 %
Protein	0.03 g.	0 %	Cholesterol	0 mg.	0 %
Carbohydrate	2.06 g.	1 %	Sodium	113 mg.	3 %

Calories From Protein: 1% Carbohydrate: 96% Fat: 3%

Dilled Garden Dip

SERVINGS: 24
SERVING SIZE: 1 Tablespoon

3/4	C.	Cottage cheese, 1% low fat
1	TBS.	Lemon juice
2	TBS.	Carrots, raw, shredded
1/2	tsp.	Dill weed
2	tsp.	Sugar or sugar substitute, Sweet'n Low
	Dash	Pepper
1	TBS.	Green onion, chopped

1. In blender container, combine cottage cheese and lemon juice. Cover; blend 2 to 3 minutes at medium speed or until smooth.

2. Stir in carrot, onion, parsley, dill, sugar and pepper. Cover; refrigerate for 2 - 3 hours. Leaving it overnight to blend flavors will give best results.

*HINT: Serve with crackers or fresh vegetables.

Nutritional Analysis

Calories	7.2	0 %	Total Fat	.08 g.	0 %
Protein	.9 g.	2 %	Cholesterol	0.31 mg.	0 %
Carbohydrate	.8 g.	0 %	Sodium	23.6 mg.	1 %

Calories from Protein: 48 %   Carbohydrate: 43 % Fat: 9 %

Egg Substitute

6	Lg.	Egg white
1/4	C.	Milk, nonfat, powdered
1	TBS.	Butter substitute, liquid

1. Combine all ingredients in a blender. Blend until smooth.

2. Keeps 1 week in refrigerator or freezer.

*NOTE: 1/4 cup substitute = 1 whole egg.

Nutritional Analysis

Calories	76	4 %	Total Fat	0.13 g.	0 %
Protein	10.6 g.	21 %	Cholesterol	0 mg.	0 %
Carbohydrate	5.9 g.	2 %	Sodium	164 mg.	5 %

Calories from Protein: 63 % Carbohydrate: 35 % Fat: 2 %

Garlic/Herb Sauce

SERVINGS: 16
SERVING SIZE: 1 Tablespoon

1	TBS.	Margarine, imitation, low fat
2	TBS.	Flour, all purpose
	Dash	Pepper
1	C.	Milk, skim
1	Med.	Garlic clove
1/2	tsp.	Basil
1/2	tsp.	Tarragon

1. In a small saucepan melt butter: Cook with garlic for 1 minute.

2. Stir in flour and pepper.

3. Add milk. Cook and stir over medium heat until thickened and bubbly.

4. Stir in basil and tarragon. Cook and stir 1 to 2 minutes more.

Nutritional Analysis

Calories	21.3	1 %	Total Fat	0.42 g.	1 %
Protein	0.65 g.	1 %	Cholesterol	0.25 mg.	0 %
Carbohydrate	1.56 g.	0 %	Sodium	15 mg.	0 %

Calories From Protein: 21% Carbohydrate: 50% Fat: 30%

Pat's Pizza Sauce

SERVINGS: 3
SERVING SIZE: 3 Cups

1 1/4	C.	Tomato puree
14	oz.	Tomato, canned, crushed
1 1/2	TBS.	Onion, minced
1	tsp.	Onion, powder
1/2	tsp.	Pepper
1/2	C.	Cheese, Parmesan, grated
3/4	TBS.	Garlic, powder
1	tsp.	Salt (optional)
1/2	tsp.	Basil

1. Mix all spices together, add both kinds of tomatoes, and mix well.

2. Refrigerate for at least 2 hours before using. The longer refrigerated the better the flavor.

*HINT: Reducing fat can be done by using a low fat parmesan cheese.

Nutritional Analysis

Calories	163	8 %	Total Fat	4.4 g.	6 %
Protein	9 g.	18 %	Cholesterol	10.7 mg.	5 %
Carbohydrate	24.3 g.	7 %	Sodium	689 mg.	21 %

Calories from protein: 21 % Carbohydrate: 56% Fat: 23 %

Salsa

SERVINGS: 6
SERVING SIZE: 1/4 Cup

PREPARATION TIME: 25 Minutes
REFRIGERATION TIME: 1 Hour

16	oz.	Tomato, canned, low sodium
1	Med.	Lime
1	Med.	Onion
3	Med.	Garlic clove, minced
1/3	Med.	Green pepper
2	tsp.	Chili powder

1. Dice onion and green pepper into small pieces. Add tomatoes, and chili powder together.

2. Squeeze lime juice into mixture.

3. Add minced garlic.

4. Mix all ingredients together and refrigerate for at least one hour. More time in refrigerator will create more flavor.

*HINTS:
- If you would like a smoother salsa, place in blender or food processor for about 10 - 15 seconds.
- Jalapeno's may be added for hotter salsa. Dice 4 Jalapeno peppers into 4 small pieces and add to mixture at step 4.

Nutritional Analysis

Calories	32	2 %	Total Fat	0.3 g.	1 %
Protein	1.3 g.	3 %	Cholesterol	0 mg.	0 %
Carbohydrate	7.4 g.	2 %	Sodium	21.6 mg.	1 %

Calories From Protein: 14% Carbohydrate: 77% Fat: 9%

Scrambled Eggs

SERVINGS: 2
SERVING SIZE: 2 Eggs

PREPARATION TIME: 10 Minutes
COOKING TIME: 10 Minutes

4	Lg.	Egg whites
2	TBS.	Green onions, chopped
	Dash	Pepper
	Dash	Salt (optional)

1. Preheat a fry pan over medium high heat.

2. Chop green onions into small pieces.

3. Separate egg whites from yolk, using only the whites. Whip whites with a fork or wire whisk.

4. Mix onions with egg whites, pepper and salt (if using).

5. Pour into a non stick skillet, and constantly stir until eggs are done. (If a buttered flavor is desired, sprinkle in about 1 teaspoon of a butter substitute while cooking).

*HINT: If a yellow color in eggs is desired, you may substitute egg beaters or the equivalent. If not available, then use 2 egg whites, and 1 whole egg. Remember this will change the Nutritional Analysis.

Nutritional Analysis

Calories	37	0 %	Total Fat	0.04 g.	0 %
Protein	7.1 g.	14 %	Cholesterol	0 mg.	0 %
Carbohydrate	1.4 g.	0 %	Sodium	1030 mg.	31 %

Calories from Protein: 83 % Carbohydrate: 16 % Fat: 1 %

ABBREVIATIONS

TEASPOON	tsp.
TABLESPOON	TBS.
CUP	C.
OUNCE	oz.
CAN	can
PACKET	pkt.
PACKAGE	pkg.
PIECES	pcs.
QUART	qt.
PINT	pt.
POUNDS	lbs.
FLUID OUNCE	fl. oz.
LARGE	lg.
MEDIUM	med.
SMALL	sm.

SUBSTITUTION GUIDE

OILS	= Applesauce or Prunes (pureed), or Butter Buds, Low fat spray, or Wonderslim	**ONION** 1 small	1 tsp. onion powder or 1 TBS. minced dry onion rehydrated
EGGS	= Egg whites, egg substitutes (2 egg whites = 1 whole egg)	**SUGAR** 1/4 C. 1/2 C.	= Sugar substitutes, or honey, juices = 3 pkt. or 1 tsp. substitute = 6 pkt. or 2 tsp. subsitute
MAYONAISE 1 C.	= Fat free mayonaise, or 1/2 C. low fat plain yogurt or 1/2 C. reduced fat mayonaise	**MUSTARD** 1 TBS.	= 1 tsp. dry
NUTS	= Grapenut cereal or substitute	**LEMON** 1 tsp.	= 1 tsp. extract
CHOCOLATE 1 square unsweetened	= 3 TBS. unsweetened cocoa + 1 TBS. butter substitute	**HARD CHEESE** 1 oz.	= 1 oz. low fat cheese or 2 TBS. grated parmesan or 1 oz. low fat processed cheese
MILK 1 C. whole	= Skim milk or non fat milk or 1 C. 1%, 2% or skim milk or 1 C. non fat cottage cheese (pureed)	**SOUR CREAM** 1 C.	= 1 C. low fat sour cream or 1 C. low fat cottage cheese
FLOUR for thickening	= Arrowroot or cornstarch	**RICOTTA CHEESE** 1 C.	= 1 C. part skim milk ricotta or 1 C. regular cottage cheese or 1 C. low fat cottage cheese
YEAST 1 Pkt. dry	= Compressed yeast or 1 cake compressed yeast	**HEAVY CREAM** 1 C.	= 1 C. half & half or 1 C. evaporated whole milk or 1 C. evaporated skim milk
BROWN SUGAR	White sugar or double amount powdered sugar	**ICE CREAM** 1 C.	= 1 C. ice milk or 1 C. sherbert or 1 C. non fat frozen yogurt
BUTTERMILK 1 C.	1 TBS. lemon juice or 1 TBS. vinegar + 1 C. skim milk	**CREAM CHEESE** 1 oz.	= 1 oz. reduced fat cream cheese or 2 TBS. low fat cream cheese (pureed)
TOMATO SAUCE 2 C.	3/4 C. tomato paste + 1 C. water	**CAKE FLOUR** 1 C.	= 1 C. minus 2 TBS. All purpose flour
GARLIC 1 clove	1/8 tsp. garlic powder or 1/8 tsp. minced dry garlic or 1/2 tsp. minced jarred garlic	**SELF RISING** **FLOUR** 1 C.	= 1 C. All purpose flour + 1/2 tsp. baking soda + 1 1/2 tsp. baking powder + 1/2 tsp. salt

CONVERSION CHARTS

DRY INGREDIENTS

1 tsp.	= 1/3 TBS.	= 1/6 fl. oz.	= 4.9 ml.
3 tsp.	= 1 TBS.	= 1/6 fl. oz.	= 14.8 ml.
2 TBS.	= 1/8 C.	= 1 fl. oz.	= 29.6 ml.
4 TBS.	= 1/4 C.	= 2 fl. oz.	= 59.1 ml.
5 1/3 TBS.	= 1/3 C.	= 2 2/3 fl. o	= 78.9 ml.
8 TBS.	= 1/2 C.	= 4 fl. oz.	= 118.3 ml.
10 2/3 TBS.	= 2/3 C.	= 5 1/3 fl. o	= 157.7 ml.
12 TBS.	= 3/4 C.	= 6 fl. oz.	= 177.4 ml.
14 TBS.	= 7/8 C.	= 7 fl. oz.	= 207.0 ml.
16 TBS.	= 1 C.	= 8 fl. oz.	= 236.6 ml.

LIQUID INGREDIENTS

1 pt.	= 2 C.	= .473 liter	= 473 ml.
1 qt.	= 2 pt.	= .946 liter	= 946 ml.
1 gallon	= 4 qt.	= 3.785 liter	= 3785 ml.
1 liter	= 1.057 qt.	= .264 gallo	= 1000 ml.

METRIC CONVERSIONS

1 g.	= .035 oz.	= .001 kg.	= 1000 mg.
1 mg.	= .001 g	= 1000 mcg.	
1 oz.	= 28.35 g. (usually rounded to 28 g.)		
1 lb.	= 16 oz.	= 453.59 g.	= .454 kg.
1 kg.	= 2.21 lb.	= 1000 g.	= 3.52 oz.

OVEN TEMPERATURES

300 F	150 C	2 mark
325 F	160 C	3 mark
350 F	180 C	4 mark
375 F	190 C	5 mark
400 F	200 C	6 mark
425 F	220 C	7 mark
450 F	230 C	8 mark
BROIL		GRILL

WATER

1 TBS.	= 15 g.	= 15 cc.
1 C.	= 237 g.	
1 fl. oz.	= 29.54 g. (usually rounded to 30 g.)	
1 cc.	= 1 g.	= 1 ml.
1 liter	= 1 kg.	= 1000 g.
1 quart	= 946 g.	= .946 kg.

PAN SIZES

9 inch round pie pan	= 22 or 23 X 4 centimeter
8 X 1 1/2 inch round cake pan	= 20 X 4 centimeter sandwich or cake pan
9 X 1/1/2 inch round cake pan	= 23 X 3.5 centimeter sandwich or cake pan
11 X 7 X 1 1/2 inch rectangle	= 28 X 18 X 4 centimeter baking pan
13 X 9 X 2 inch rectangle	= 32.5 X 23 X 5 centimeter baking pan
12 X 7 1/2 X 2 inch rectangle	= 30 X 19 X 5 centimeter baking pan
15 X 10 X 2 inch rectangle	= 38 X 25 X 2.5 centimeter baking pan
9 X 5 X 3 inch loaf	= 23 X 13 X 6 centimeter baking or loaf pan

INDEX

PASTA AND RICE

VEGETABLE DISHES

SWEETS AND SNACKS

SWEET AND SNACKS CONT.

BEVERAGES

SAUCES, DIPS, AND MISC.

ORDER PAGE

ITEM	QTY	PRICE	TOTAL
A NEW YOU Cookbook: (Includes tools)	_____	@ $17.95	_____
Tools: Laminated Shopping list with pen. Laminated Conversion chart, and Substitute guide.	_____	@ $ 6.95	
Sugar Free Chocolates:			
Milk Chocolate	_____	@ $ 6.95	_____
Semi-Sweet Chocolate	_____	@ $ 6.95	_____
White	_____	@ $ 6.95	_____
Apron: A NEW YOU or "Baked with Love in (your Name) Kitchen"	_____	@ $ 21.95	_____
Recipe Modification or Analysis: (per recipe, more than one is $ 3.75 per recipe)	_____	@ $5.00	_____
Restaurant Menu Nutrition Brochures & Analysis:		Price subject to job	

POSTAGE: _____
($4.95 S&H)

TOTAL: _____

Questions, more information or Comments
Write or Call:

Physiques Publications, P.O. Box 1555, Beaverton, OR 97075
(503) 626-5168